ENJOY A FULL YEAR

FREE

Thanks for adding *Budget Backyard Makeovers* to your library of do-it-yourself books! The editors of *Backyard Living* have compiled the best of the best tips and ideas to inspire you to create a more beautiful backyard—all on a shoestring budget. And now, you can keep these helpful, easy (and affordable!) tips and ideas coming to your home all year long— **FREE!** Here's how.

$23.94 VALUE

backyard living

FREE SUBSCRIPTION CARD

101+ homegrown ideas & tips
TOP TOMATO TIPS
new & improved!

backyard living

NEW IDEAS FOR container gardens

Grandma's Best Growing Secrets

20 TIPS FOR gardeners on the go

WIN THIS $13,000 TRACTOR!

FRESH PLANT COMBOS THAT GET NOTICED

TURN THRIFTY FINDS INTO TREASURES

8 SIMPLE WAYS TO UPDATE YOUR DECK

Return this card today to claim your Free 1-Year Subscription (a $23.94 value) to *Backyard Living* magazine. You'll enjoy an entire year of easy, time-saving— and affordable—backyard projects delivered to your home, along with instant access to our exclusive website, www.BackyardLivingMagazine.com.

YES! PLEASE START MY **FREE SUBSCRIPTION** TO *BACKYARD LIVING* MAGAZINE!

NAME _____
(please print)

ADDRESS _____

CITY _____

STATE _____ ZIP _____

E-MAIL _____

Backyard Living is published 6 times per year at the annual cover price of $23.94. Please allow 4-6 weeks for delivery of your first FREE issue.

DETACH HERE & MAIL TODAY!

QI0BAF1Ń

MAIL THIS CARD TODAY!

Discover 101+ Homegrown Ideas in Every Issue with Your FREE YEAR of *Backyard Living!*

As a *Backyard Living* subscriber, you'll look forward to:

- **100+ Full-Color Photos** that'll inspire and motivate you to a more beautiful yard

- **Easy-To-Do, Step-By-Step Projects** you can take on…and accomplish

- **"Trade Secrets"** and professional know-how from our own Plant Doctor

- **Top 10 Lists** of "must-have" plants and flowers for your landscaping

- **Instant Access to Our Exclusive Website** packed with more easy, <u>affordable</u> tips, ideas and projects for a more beautiful backyard

Send for your FREE YEAR today!

SUBSCRIPTION FULFILLMENT CENTER
PO BOX 5502
HARLAN IA 51593-1002

budget
backyard makeovers

GET DAZZLING RESULTS ON A SHOESTRING BUDGET!

BIRDS & BLOOMS

BIRDS & BLOOMS BOOKS · REIMAN MEDIA GROUP, INC. · GREENDALE, WISCONSIN

BIRDS & BLOOMS

A *BIRDS & BLOOMS/READER'S DIGEST* BOOK

Editor: Deb Warlaumont Mulvey
Art Director: Nicholas Mork
Contributing Editors: Teri Dunn, Rachael Liska
Contributing Art Director: Sharon Nelson
Graphic Art Associate: Ellen Lloyd
Associate Layout Designer: Julie Stone
Contributing Layout Designer: Kathy Crawford
Copy Editor: Susan Uphill
Editorial Assistant: Crystal Rennicke
Digital Illustrations: Robert Gaszak
Graphic Art Intern: Heather Metz

Senior Editor, Retail Books: Jennifer Olski
Creative Director: Ardyth Cope
Editor, *Birds & Blooms*: Heather Lamb
Vice President, Executive Editor/Books: Heidi Reuter Lloyd
Editor in Chief, Home and Garden: Jeff Nowak
President, Home and Garden and Health and Wellness: Alyce C. Alston
President and Chief Executive Officer: Mary G. Berner

Pictured on front cover:
Beth Grader's garden in Marblehead, Massachusetts (pp. 40-43); photo by Gary Mottau

International Standard Book Number (10): 0-89821-650-8
International Standard Book Number (13): 978-089821-650-9

For other *Birds & Blooms* books and products, visit *www.birdsandblooms.com*.
For more *Reader's Digest* products and information,
visit *www.rd.com* (in the United States)
www.rd.ca (in Canada)

Printed in China
1 3 5 7 9 10 8 6 4 2

contents

GET DAZZLING RESULTS ON A SHOESTRING BUDGET!

CHAPTER 1

small spaces | 6

No room to garden? Guess again. Here's how to make the most of even the smallest space.

CHAPTER 2

water gardens | 30

Yes, you can afford a water garden! Learn how from homeowners who built their own.

CHAPTER 5

extreme makeovers | 126

These homeowners took on Mother Nature...and won! Learn the secrets to their successes.

CHAPTER 6

heaven on earth | 156

You, too, can create your own paradise. All you need is elbow grease...and a dream.

(plan) HERE'S THE
••Check out detailed plans for 36 gardens, starting on page 11.

BONUS SECTION!

backyard planning kit | 193

Get started today with these expert tips and no-fail garden plans.

small
spaces

welcome
TO PAULAVILLE

SHE CREATED A BACKYARD HAVEN...IN 900 SQUARE FEET.

PAULA VIETMEIER
CANONSBURG, PENNSYLVANIA

When Rob and Paula Vietmeier moved into their new home southwest of Pittsburgh, their backyard didn't have so much as a blade of grass. Twelve years later, it looks like a small botanical garden.

Rob provided the muscle for the project, hauling plants, pickup truckloads of mulch, and enlisting friends to help him dig a pond. But the design is all Paula's.

"Our friends and relatives call it 'Paulaville,'" she laughs.

Her plan for transforming the 900-square-foot backyard in Canonsburg, Pennsylvania started simply—with rocks. Builders left behind a pile of boulders from the home's foundation, so Paula had a bulldozer operator space four of them evenly across the back of the lot.

"I just knew I could build around them and make it look nice," she says. "One even has a nice bowl shape. It fills up with water, and the birds use it as a bath."

A PERFECT HIDEAWAY

After putting in the lawn, Paula and Rob built a deck over the walkout basement. Paula also wanted a "garden room" with a swing beneath the deck, so she and Rob began laying pavers for the patio.

"That was the hardest thing we've ever done," Paula says. "We put in a base of gravel, then a base of sand, and started laying pavers. It was almost complete when we learned we should tamp the pavers down, so we rented a power tamper.

"We started in the middle...mistake number one. Mistake number two...we didn't have the border in place yet. It was like walking on

an unfinished puzzle on a carpet. Everything just exploded and we had to start over."

Once the patio was complete, Paula got back to planting, creating a circular perennial garden that became the centerpiece of the yard.

"I saw a big circle garden overflowing with flowers in a magazine and loved it," she says. "Rob put a peg in the ground, attached a string, then walked in a circle with a can of spray paint to outline the grass we needed to dig up."

Paula edged the garden with handpicked stones from a brickyard. It wasn't long before it became her favorite place to shop.

but it blocks some of the wind."

The Vietmeiers planted a weeping cherry, rhododendrons, hostas and ferns in front of the fence.

"I love the woodland effect the ferns create in late summer, when they're large and lush," Paula says. "It gives the garden a cool feeling even on a hot day."

To finish off the landscape, Rob and some friends dug out a 99-gallon pond.

PERFECT FOR ENTERTAINING

"This pond is just the right size for our small backyard, and it's a great source of entertain-

"I love the woodland effect the ferns create

Paula edged this pond with rocks unearthed during the construction of her home.

BUDGET SECRET:

Come up with your own designs. Paula browses through catalogs to choose plants, then makes photo collages to see how certain plants look together.

$

"I'd stop there after work and fill up my trunk with rocks and boulders," she says. "Everything was sold by the ton, so a trunkload was only $4 or $5."

PICK OF THE PLANTS

Paula chose most of her plants from garden catalogs, selecting flowers with different bloom times to ensure continuous color. To help them stand out, Paula and Rob installed a 12-foot fence as a backdrop.

"We bought a stockade fence, took it apart and then put it back together, skipping every other picket so it looks more open," Paula says. "The fence doesn't enclose the yard or seal it off,

ment," Paula says. "It attracts a few frogs every year, and we love seeing the birds that come to cool off in the fountain spray."

When the Vietmeiers invite friends, Paula floats candles on the water and strings white lights around the pond, through the plants and over the arbor. Guests relax in the 10- by 16-foot garden room, which overflows with hanging baskets and houseplants. A lattice twined with wisteria provides shade.

"Often, I spend the whole evening playing in the yard," Paula says. "It'll be dark when Rob calls for me, telling me it's time to come in, just like my mom did when I was a kid." ❧

HERE'S THE plan

1. Water garden
2. Ferns
3. Arbor
4. Climbing roses
5. Rose garden
6. Hosta
7. Boulder
8. Daylily
9. Hemlock
10. Birdbath
11. Weeping cherry
12. Hydrangea
13. Garden room
14. Sundial
15. Aster
16. Bellflower
17. Clara Curtis mum
18. Lemon fluff
19. Shasta daisy
20. Yarrow
21. Carnation
22. Astilbe

in late summer, when they're **large and lush.**"

BUDGET SECRET:

Start with a focal point. Paula started with four boulders, "and everything took off from there."

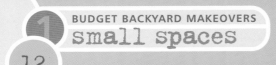

east MEETS west

THIS SMALL ASIAN GARDEN GIVES THE ILLUSION OF A MUCH LARGER SPACE.

DAN AND VICKY FRICKLE
OTIS ORCHARDS, WASHINGTON

A peek over the fence into Dan and Vicky Frickle's tranquil garden retreat is like a trip halfway around the world.

From the sculpted juniper to the hand-painted Chinese mural adorning the cedar fence, this compact space in eastern Washington, just outside Spokane, has the exotic feel of the Orient.

The Frickles' Asian-inspired oasis in Otis Orchards makes the most of a small space, but they didn't start this project by choice. Mother Nature thrust it upon them.

"When a root fungus claimed one of our beloved white pines, we were suddenly left with an unsightly blank corner of our yard," Dan recalls. "Although it was a sad day, it also gave us a fresh opportunity to plan the garden we always wanted. Now, the location was handed to us."

Inspired by their interest in a Far East-flavored garden in a nearby city park, Dan bought a book on Asian gardens and started planning.

"For weeks, I thought about what we should do," he says. "Then I woke up one morning with a crystal-clear vision of the entire garden design. A quick pencil sketch, some cedar boards and a few landscaping blocks later, we were ready to tackle what would become a 3-month project."

Dan's daughter's boyfriend, Brian Williams, pitched in and the two constructed a simple but sturdy 5- by 6-foot deck. Once that was built, they moved it to cover the remaining tree stump. A couple of coats of deck stain brought the platform to life.

With the deck in place, it was time to bring in the Far East theme.

"We looked in garden shops for large bamboo poles, but had no luck," Dan says. "Brian works at a fence-post manufacturing company, so he brought me several pine posts of varying diameters, which we cut to various lengths. We screwed them onto the corners of the deck to resemble bamboo."

Curved, raised flower beds made from landscaping blocks lead visitors further into the garden. The Frickles

They didn't start this project by choice. Mother Nature thrust it upon them.

used flat river rock from northern Idaho to create the edging, then paved the walking areas with pea gravel.

The garden beds are planted with a variety of hostas, ferns, ornamental grasses and impatiens. A showy fuchsia and unique bat-face plant, as well as a crimson-leaved Japanese maple, add just the right amount of color.

"We tried to plant things that we thought would stay fairly small," Dan explains. "The garden lends itself to plants that can be pinched back and manicured." One challenging idea was taming an overgrown 25-year-old juniper in bonsai style.

FINISHING TOUCHES

Like many Asian gardens, this one features an arched bridge as a centerpiece.

"Ideally, we wanted a concrete or stone bridge to span the dry steam bed, but we couldn't find anything small enough for our area with that Eastern flair," Dan says. "I created my own from cedar strips, a sheet of 3/4-inch plywood and lots of deck screws." ❦

(in progress)

LOCATION OF
WHITE PINE
STUMP ·········▶

BUDGET SECRET:

If you can't find bamboo poles for your Asian-themed garden, substitute pine posts of different diameters and cut them to various lengths. Use pressure-treated wood to prevent rot. **$**

HERE'S THE plan

1. Fern
2. Hosta
3. Japanese maple
4. Low-voltage lighting
5. Pagoda
6. Gong
7. Ornamental grass
8. Log steps
9. Fuchsia
10. Juniper
11. Impatiens
12. Barberry
13. Bat-face plant
14. Apple tree
15. Fountain
16. Jacob's ladder

MAKING
an entrance

INEXPENSIVE ACCENTS ADD PIZZAZZ TO THIS FRONT YARD.

We have several flower gardens in our yard, but the small bed near our front door is the most rewarding. This colorful garden was really fun to create, offers a cheery welcome to our guests and brings in lots of compliments from friends and family. Best of all, it didn't cost much!

My "exterior decorating" project started when I bought an 8-foot section of 4-foot-tall fence from a local building-supply store. It made a great backdrop for the birdbath garden we had in our front yard. It also inspired me to add other accents to this half-circle plot.

DECORATIVE TOUCHES

A pretty vine wreath—made from branches trimmed from the creeping vine on the side of our home—surrounds a "welcome" plaque we placed on the fence above the birdbath.

Two wicker wall baskets that I picked up at a garage sale are filled with vinca vine and pansies.

I recycled a small step stool to use as a plant holder and placed an old red carpenter's box on it. The box is divided into four sections, and each holds a clay pot of wax begonias.

I think the floppy straw hat on one corner of the fence and the watering cans used as accent pieces contribute more charm. And I've added other decorative touches, including garden signs and a rustic birdhouse.

BY ROSEMARY WEAVER GARNER, IOWA

BE CREATIVE

To plant the garden itself, I used a combination of seeds and bedding plants. Bedding plants quickly produce colorful results, but seeds are more economical—especially for gardeners who plant as many beds as I do.

With a little imagination, you can turn almost any area of your yard—no matter how small—into an inviting spot. ❧

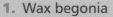

$ BUDGET SECRET: Recycle vintage items like watering cans and wicker baskets as accent pieces.

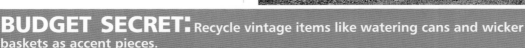

1. Wax begonia
2. Ageratum
3. Moss rose
4. Salvia
5. Snapdragon
6. Petunia
7. California poppy
8. Morning glory
9. Celosia
10. Four-o' clock
11. Johnny jump-ups
12. Hosta
13. Chrysanthemum

HERE'S THE

NEW FRAME of mind

AN UNUSUAL FOCAL POINT TURNED THIS POSTAGE-STAMP LOT INTO A STUNNING RETREAT.

BY PAUL AND DEANNA MYERS
MERIDIAN, IDAHO

Our landscape challenge began when we moved to a newly developed neighborhood with compact lots. The only green space around our home was a postage-stamp front lawn and a long, narrow side yard that resembled a 14- by 70-foot bandage.

The view in front didn't bother my wife, Deanna, and me. But the side yard was another story. It faced the plain two-story wall of the neighboring house, which featured assorted windows, dryer vents and a fireplace chimney.

(before)

BUDGET SECRET:

$

No money for building supplies? Find 'em on the cheap. Lena and Mike Jascur of Flora, Indiana salvage wood for garden structures when their neighbors tear down old barns and sheds.

From blah to beautiful: Suspended window frames, a mosaic of groundcovers, and heron sculptures flanking a stone fountain worked wonders. An elegant seating area (top) sits across from the lighted columns.

BUDGET SECRET:

Want free rocks? Check with farmers in your area. Pat and Ron Gossman of Fairview, Pennsylvania collected more than 5,000 stones from farmers to build paths and ponds.

$

Although our yard came fully "landscaped," according to the builder, the side yard featured only the basics–rolled-out sod, miscellaneous plants and shrubs, and a concrete pad for a patio. To top it off, the soil underneath was heavy clay, virtually guaranteeing that nothing would thrive. Something had to be done, and it was time to roll up our sleeves and take charge.

NEW FOCUS

My first priority was creating a focal point for our narrow side yard, one that would draw the eye upward. And because we like to relax outdoors in the evening, adding lighting was high on the priority list.

Meanwhile, Deanna was busy planning flower beds. Her personal view is that there can never be too many blooms. So most of our grass had to go.

We did discover there can be too many great ideas for a small yard. We had to be extra hard on our design and diligently edit our ideas to avoid a crowded, hodgepodge landscape.

After lots of discussion, we finally got the mix right on paper and got to work.

I tackled my concept for the focal point by building four tapered wooden columns and connecting them to a 22-foot beam that I positioned directly across from the patio. To finish it, I suspended window frames from the beam and hung large planters inside each window, creating what is essentially living art.

The design broke up the stark walls of the neighbor's house and gave us something beautiful to look at.

COLUMNS OF LIGHT

The columns themselves look solid, but they're actually hollow three-sided pieces with open backs that I used to add garden lighting. I mounted a 40-watt bulb in each to brighten the whole structure. When the lights are turned on, they provide a wash of gold color on the neighbor's wall, adding depth and atmosphere.

The next phase involved removing the lawn so we'd have room for a rustic stone path and flower beds. I still have to mow a tiny section, which I kept so we have a place to play with our grandsons.

The only other item that needed to be built was a 7-foot-long fence to screen our air conditioner. After we installed it, we discovered a hidden benefit. The back side was the perfect place for us to place a potting bench.

TIME TO PLANT

With the path laid and flower beds carved

A rustic stone path takes a leisurely route to the backyard.

"It's almost like we

out, we were ready to put in as many plants as possible. That's when we noticed the yard's extreme lighting conditions–a mix of strong, hot sunlight followed by deep shade. Plants that needed lots of bright light were out. Still, with a little guidance, we found we had plenty of flowers and shrubs to choose from.

HERE'S THE plan

1. Dogwood
2. Birdbath
3. Sand cherry
4. Bleeding heart
5. Firethorn
6. Coralbells
7. Astilbe
8. Hydrangea
9. Sweet woodruff
10. Thyme
11. Ajuga
12. Creeping Jenny
13. Window boxes
14. Container gardens
15. Clay fireplace
16. Rhododendron
17. Delphinium
18. Potting bench
19. Euonymus
20. Tomatoes

A mix of silver and green foliage produced a **luxuriant** crazy-quilt design.

For height and privacy, we planted a pair of 'Prairie Fire' crabapple trees at each end of the yard. To anchor different areas of the garden, we used shrubs like photinia, burning bush, dogwood and butterfly bush. Then we filled in with dwarf rhododendron, hosta, astilbe, ever-blooming hydrangea, bleeding heart, violet, delphinium, pansy and coralbells.

Deanna's vision for the bed in front of the columns included a small stone fountain flanked by iron sculptures of blue herons and surrounded by a mosaic of groundcovers. We turned to sweet woodruff, creeping Jenny, dusty miller, creeping thyme, bugleweed and a variegated dwarf euonymus. The result: a lush silver-and-green crazy-quilt design.

NATURAL ADDITIONS

For more ambiance, we looked to add more than just greenery to the backyard. We positioned a pretty birdbath and several small boulders along the path, as well as a table and bench. We also added an attractive clay outdoor fireplace to the

added an **extra room** onto our house!"

patio and softened the wall behind it with a window box filled with coleus, impatiens and other shade-tolerant plants.

Now we have a lush hideaway that feels cozy yet spacious and looks manicured but comfortable. It's almost like we added an extra room onto our house!

When Deanna and I enjoy our lovely southwest Idaho evenings outside, we're warmed by the crackle of the fire and the burnished glow in our little but lovely backyard. ✳

BUDGET SECRET:

$ Instead of building a structure to hide an eyesore, install an inexpensive trellis and let vining plants cover it.

PLENTY OF
room to bloom

WITH JUST A TINY PATIO, SHE CREATED A BACKYARD THAT'S BIG ON BLOSSOMS.

It's only natural to have big aspirations when it comes to gardening. But what if your available space resembles a window box more than a grand botanical garden?

> **"I don't believe you should have a garden without a spot to relax."**

With the right plants and structures, even small spaces can become great gardens, whether you're dealing with a modest yard or simply want to pack more pow around your patio.

Laurie Morgan looked for several seasons of color when planning for her small garden.

"I carefully pick and choose my plants so there's always something blooming," she says.

Although Laurie's former home in Greendale, Wisconsin had a very limited planting space—just 25 by 30 feet—she still found room to incorporate a couple of cozy chairs in addition to 24 different types of plants.

"I don't believe you should have a garden without a spot to relax in," she reflects. "It's nice to have a place to observe the yard—even if it's just watching the bees work."

Need some more ideas for sprucing up your small space? Consider these pointers from Laurie:

- **Foundation plantings** are a good start, but don't stop there. Containers are a quick and easy way to add **bright flowers** anywhere, especially soil-free areas like porches and patios.

- In tight quarters, gardeners need to **make every inch count**, so it helps to plan the landscape in layers. Start at ground level and work your way up, envisioning a way to fill each tier of visual space with plants—low groundcovers, mid-sized perennials and annuals, and taller shrubs and trees.

- For the illusion of a **larger garden**, double up—mix bulbs with perennials, and annuals with shrubs. Placing different plants in the same location makes it easier to **create year-round interest** in less space.

- Include **evergreens** to add structure. Many dwarf varieties are perfect for smaller landscapes, including dwarf Alberta spruce, Fat Albert blue spruce and Nootka false cypress.

BUDGET SECRET:

Make the most of a limited budget by buying plants that will multiply on their own, like creeping phlox and daffodils. Allow them some elbow room at planting time so they have space to spread out.

HERE'S THE plan

1. Yew
2. Japanese anemone
3. Climbing rose
4. Sweet autumn clematis
5. Daffodil
6. Boxwood
7. Rose
8. Baptisia
9. Tulip
10. Pasque flower
11. Phlox
12. Grape hyacinth
13. Salvia
14. Sedum
15. Nierembergia
16. Creeping phlox
17. Sweet alyssum
18. Ageratum
19. Lavender
20. Germander
21. Chives

antique look,
BUDGET PRICE

COMPACT FAUX-STONE
POTS MAKE AN
ENDURING IMPRESSION.

BY AMBER COOK, REDMOND, WASHINGTON

All gardeners have their fantasies, and one of mine has always been to have a porch display of centuries-old stone garden pots.

But antiques like that are hard to find, and if I could find them, they certainly wouldn't fit my budget.

So, I make my own. They're small, so a grouping makes a tiny gardening space seem a lot bigger. And they evoke the rich past, just like real stone pots.

The first stone pots were made of volcanic rock. European stone carvers cut the rock into blocks to build French castles, Italian villas, and sinks and troughs for European cottages.

In the early 1900s, resourceful English gardeners discovered these old basins made perfect planters. As the limited supply of original pots dwindled, the Brits created their own stone pots. Now you can, too.

After creating your own "antique," you may want to get creative and add a few personal touches. Here's how:

Weather it. After the pot dries, brush the edges for a more realistic aged-stone appearance. For best results, use a wire brush held at an angle. This will deepen the cracks, folds and shadows.

Add color. As you mix the cement, add a small amount of cement color additive powder. I like the soft pastel-pink look.

Enhance with moss. Cut moss into small pieces and blend or beat into buttermilk. Pat the mix over the outside of the planter, set it aside and watch the moss grow in 2 to 3 weeks.

Of course, one of the best ways to individualize your patio pots is with your plant choices. Select plants that do well in shallow soil. From there, you'll be on your way to an instant classic! 🌿

WHAT YOU NEED:

- ☐ Rubber gloves
- ☐ Peat moss
- ☐ Perlite
- ☐ Portland cement
- ☐ Plastic tub
- ☐ Sand
- ☐ 24" by 24" board
- ☐ 24" by 24" plastic sheet (medium weight)

1 Wearing rubber gloves, mix two parts peat moss with one part perlite in a plastic tub. Add one part portland cement and mix with water until it's the consistency of cottage cheese.

2 Make a pile of wet sand (about as much as you can hold in your cupped hands) and place it on top of the board. Pat sand into a mound. Cover with the plastic sheet. Scoop cement mixture on and around the covered sand pile and pat into your container's shape.

3 Gather the plastic sheet in one hand and pat the mix from the outside to shape the pot. Gently tilt the pot away from the board and pack wet sand under the edges. Unfold the plastic, flatten a small area on the bottom of the pot, and add drainage holes. Let your pot dry for 2 or 3 days.

EDITOR'S NOTE: Because concrete has a high lime content, these pots may be harmful or toxic to some plants, especially acid-loving ones. To prevent plant damage, leave pots outdoors for a few weeks. A few good soaking rainfalls will leach the lime away.

BRIGHTideas

OFF TO THE SIDE
Set against architectural elements like arbors, fences and walls, the right plants will make narrow side yards shine.

dead space comes to life This 7- by 30-foot side yard wasn't much to look at until Charlotte Graham transformed it into a showcase. "It was just dead space," says Charlotte of Pittsboro, Indiana. "But it got a lot of sun, and I thought the arborvitae along the lot line would provide a nice backdrop for a cottage garden." Husband Rex built the elegant arbor, which Charlotte designed to echo the gables on their house.

retirement benefits Gloria Higgs of Arlington, Texas says her husband took up landscaping as a retirement hobby. Now this cozy corner, with its vine-covered arbor and tidy plantings, is one of her favorite spots. Purple-flowered lilyturf thrives in the shade beneath the meticulously pruned crape-myrtle trees. "The patio is a haven to enjoy any time of day, whether we're having our morning coffee or watching the birds," Gloria says.

urban renewal

Some residents might not even bother trying to plant in a space this tight, but imagine how bleak this streetscape would be without the sunflowers and daylilies to soften the iron fence. Bright petunias spilling from window boxes draw the eye upward, making the space seem larger. Leslie Harrison photographed this scene near her condominium in Hoboken, New Jersey.

PACKED PATIOS

Tight quarters? Rest easy. If you have room for a lawn chair, you have room for flowers.

lovely layers Layering is an ideal way to cram lots of color into small spaces like patios. Ann and Dale Johnston of Thousand Oaks, California transformed a long, narrow yard by edging their patio with tons of hanging baskets and containers. Dale's tip: Position the containers so any excess water from the hanging baskets can drip into the pots beneath them.

thinking big This flower-packed Eureka, California backyard consists of a 600-square-foot patio—but it looks much bigger. Owners Joseph and Mary Stemach achieve this illusion by surrounding the patio with flowers. Combining low planters in front with taller pots and suspended baskets creates a sense of depth and disguises the backyard's boundary while suggesting an even larger garden beyond it.

scale it down When space is limited, there's no need to do things on a grand scale. Instead of installing an entire fence, buy just one section and plan a miniature garden around it to create a scaled-down focal point. Kristie Statz of Cross Plains, Wisconsin used fence sections to dress up her front yard. This straight section anchors the center of the yard, and corner sections define the edges.

SMALL SPACE, BIG IMPACT

Look on the bright side: Small spaces make it easier to create a focal point or play up an attractive feature.

reflect on this Believe it or not, this photo shows the *reflection* of a backyard garden. Larry and Sue Lapp of Ozark, Alabama came up with this clever and economical idea. They removed the glass from old window frames, replaced it with mirrors, and hung the frames on the back of their garage, where they would reflect the prettiest view of their garden. "It's a nice effect, and the 'view' is different each time we look at it," Sue says.

COMPACT KNOCKOUTS FOR
TIGHT QUARTERS

PANSY
VIOLA X WITTROCKIANA

Bloom time: Spring to summer.

Hardiness: Annual; can be grown anywhere.

Light needs: Full sun to partial shade.

Mature plant size: 6 to 9 inches high and wide.

Care tip: These plants prefer some shade. Provide extra water during hot spells.

LADY'S MANTLE
ALCHEMILLA MOLLIS

Bloom time: Late spring to early summer.

Hardiness: Zones 4 to 8.

Light needs: Full sun; also does well in partial shade.

Mature plant size: 1 to 2 feet high and wide.

Care tip: Provide fertile, well-drained soil in sun or shade.

FLOWERING MAPLE
ABUTILON SPECIES

Bloom time: All summer.

Hardiness: Zone 9 and 10; grown as an annual or houseplant in colder areas.

Light needs: Full to partial sun.

Mature plant size: 3 to 5 feet high, 3 to 4 feet wide.

Care tip: Pinch stems back to keep plant in bounds and encourage bushier growth.

'EASY WAVE' PINK PETUNIA
PETUNIA X HYBRIDA 'EASY WAVE'

Bloom time: All summer.

Hardiness: Annual; can be grown anywhere.

Light needs: Full sun.

Mature plant size: 1 foot high, 1 to 3 feet wide.

Care tip: 'Wave' petunias weather heat and tolerate neglect, but good care produces truly impressive plants.

JAPANESE PAINTED FERN
ATHYRIUM NIPONICUM 'PICTUM'

Bloom time: Grown for foliage.

Hardiness: Zones 5 to 8.

Light needs: Partial to full shade; can tolerate part-day sun.

Mature plant size: 1 to 2 feet high, 1 foot wide.

Care tip: It's considered a shade plant, but the gorgeous coloration intensifies with a little more sun.

TOO-LARGE PLANTS CAN MAKE A SMALL GARDEN LOOK EVEN SMALLER. THESE COMPACT PLANTS PRODUCE BEAUTIFUL COLOR AT A REASONABLE PRICE—AND YOU CAN COUNT ON THEM TO STAY IN BOUNDS.

CALIBRACHOA

CALIBRACHOA HYBRIDS, INCLUDING 'MILLION BELLS', 'SUPERBELLS', 'LIRICASHOWERS', 'CELEBRATION' AND 'COLORBURST'

Bloom time: All summer.

Hardiness: Annual; can be grown anywhere.

Light needs: Full to partial sun.

Mature plant size: 10 to 15 inches high, 20 to 30 inches wide.

Care tip: The trailing habit is ideal for w indow boxes; deadheading is not necessary.

LAVENDER

LAVANDULA ANGUSTIFOLIA 'HIDCOTE'

Bloom time: All summer.

Hardiness: Zones 5 to 9.

Light needs: Full sun.

Mature plant size: 12 to 15 inches high, 12 inches wide.

Care tip: Grow in sandy, gravelly soil. Lavender needs good drainage and slightly alkaline conditions to thrive.

MAIDEN PINK

DIANTHUS DELTOIDES 'ZING ROSE'

Bloom time: Late spring to early summer.

Hardiness: Zones 4 to 9.

Light needs: Full sun.

Mature plant size: 8 to 10 inches high and wide.

Care tip: If you cut back plants after blooming, they often muster an encore performance.

FEVERFEW

TANACETUM PARTHENIUM

Bloom time: All summer.

Hardiness: Zones 5 to 9.

Light needs: Full sun.

Mature plant size: 2 to 3 feet high and wide.

Care tip: With full sun, this plant is is easy to grow in any soil, in a pot or in the ground.

CORALBELLS

HEUCHERA CULTIVARS

Bloom time: Spring to summer.

Hardiness: Zones 4 to 9.

Light needs: Full sun to partial shade..

Mature plant size: 1 to 3 feet high, 1 foot wide.

Care tip: Organically rich soil and partial shade are ideal.

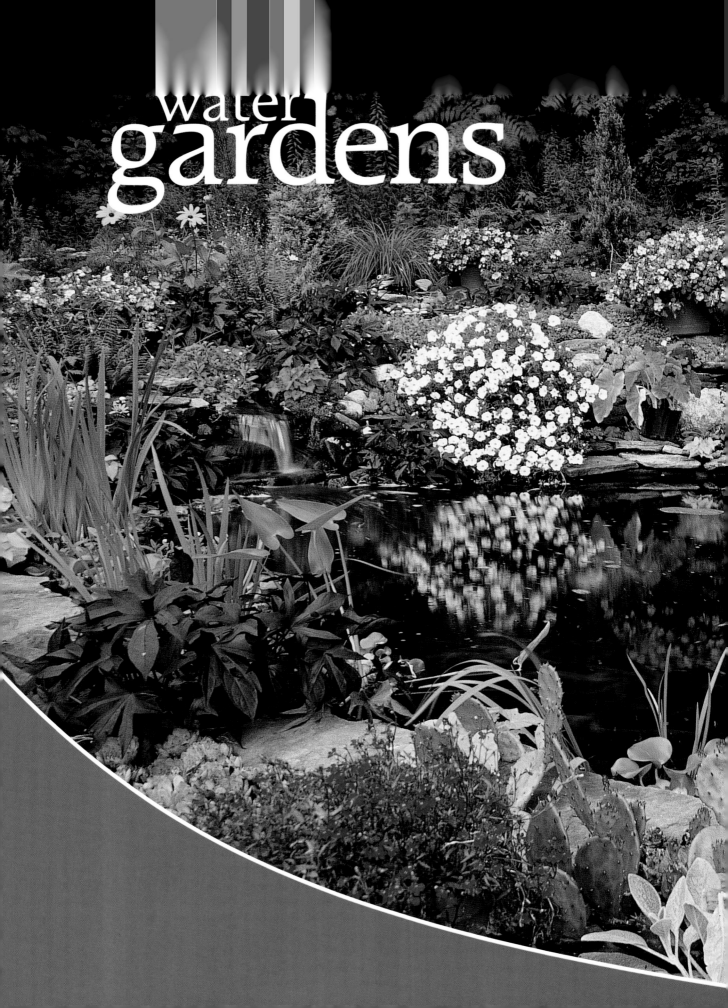

water
gardens

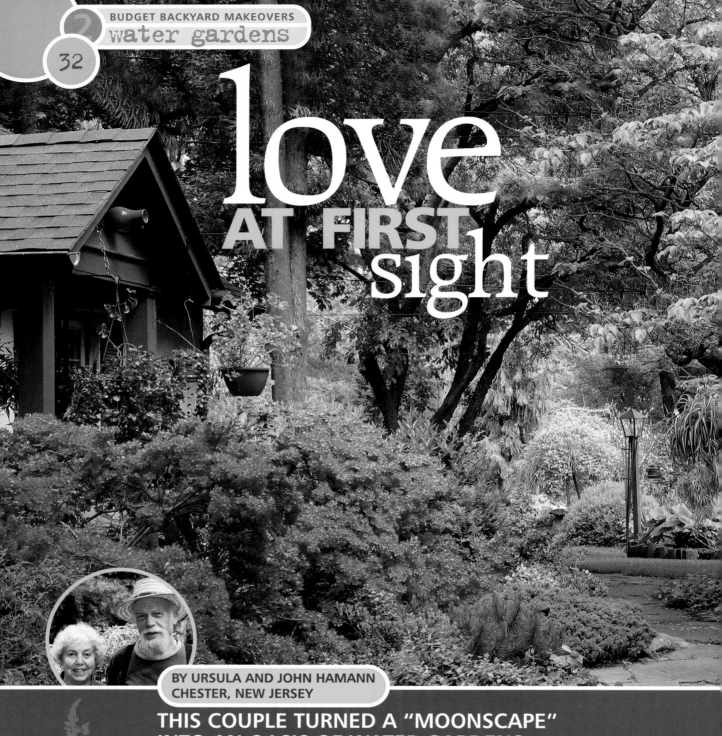

love
AT FIRST
sight

**BY URSULA AND JOHN HAMANN
CHESTER, NEW JERSEY**

THIS COUPLE TURNED A "MOONSCAPE" INTO AN OASIS OF WATER GARDENS.

I'll never forget standing in the living room of the empty cottage with my husband, John, and watching the real estate agent stride toward the large picture window. With a dramatic gesture, she hurled back the drapes, revealing a wintry landscape of fields, woods and rolling hills.

It looked like a barren moonscape, yet there was something so right about it. For us, it was perfect. John and I have called this northern New Jersey cottage home for more than 40 years.

It was 1954, and I'd just left my family in Germany to embark on a new life, persuaded by love and the spirit of youth. Little did I know this fertile homestead awaited across the Atlantic.

After the snow melted, I went on my first "treasure hunt" in our new yard. A cluster of cro-

BUDGET SECRET: $

A liner pad protects your pond liner from rocks, so it can be a worthwhile investment. But there's a cheaper alternative. Tom and Martha Loveless of Glasgow, Kentucky used old carpet padding. It worked just as well as an expensive liner—but didn't cost a dime.

cuses welcomed me. Walking around got my head spinning with ideas. Preoccupations with establishing a lush, green lawn soon were overshadowed by more creative gardening endeavors.

A ROCKY START

With pick and shovel, I started our backyard transformation with the two stone- and weed-infested embankments flanking our driveway. After bringing in new topsoil, I shaped the area into terraces for a rock garden.

Along these banks I also built a 20- by 30-inch cement birdbath. I loved it, and promised myself a bigger and better pond in the future.

John and I made good on that promise in 1963, when we built our first water garden. Working from my sketch, he assembled a form for a 650-gallon water garden from sheet metal and wire, which we covered with concrete and sealed with epoxy paint. It wasn't as easy as using today's pond liners, but it worked.

Inspired by the area's native limestone, we wanted to add a natural-looking waterfall. A farmer sympathetic to our cause extended a generous offer: We had 1 day to remove as many rocks from his land as we wanted, at no charge. We slept well that night!

Once the waterfall was in place, the land seemed to come to life. We surrounded it with pines and shrubs, creating shelter for many birds. I can even remember spying the first frog. It was sunning itself on a carpet of thyme next to the water's edge. What else did I need?

We were hooked on the lively beauty the water garden gave our landscape. Soon we were scouting a site for another pond.

We chose a shady spot adjacent to a barn John had built. He began outlining the future waterlily

BUDGET SECRET:

Natural materials make a water feature look like it's been there forever—and they're free. "Items native to your area are easier to find, and blend in with your backyard," says Donna Evans of North Mankato, Minnesota. "We used limestone, which is common around here. We found all the free rocks we needed at road-construction projects." $

pond with a garden hose. By spring of 1989, another boring part of the lawn had been taken over by tranquil reflections.

Since it was on a gentle slope, this pond needed careful digging—water always responds to gravity—and an extended flower garden to link it to the landscape. I planted iris, black-eyed Susan, Joe Pye weed, daylily, aster, yarrow and phlox, plus evergreens, hydrangea, weeping pussy willow and tall bamboo.

We're just as excited about our backyard now as we were when we got that first glimpse through the picture window. Sometimes we surprise ourselves with our endless enthusiasm for more gardening projects.

When I needed space for some bearded irises, John used his tiller to widen a border near the end of our garden. We cleared an area of about 2,300 square feet flanked by tall pines and a forsythia jungle. Before we knew it, the garden hose was out, and we were outlining our third water feature.

This time, I wanted to incorporate a charming brook to remind me of my childhood memories of Germany. There I was, at 72, shaping

> **"There I was, at 72,** shaping a brook out of wire mesh, cement and river rock!"

a brook out of wire mesh, cement and river rock! John concealed the filtering system by covering it with broken flagstone pieces, which made the brook look natural.

When we look at our gardens from the front picture window now, the word "barren" doesn't come to mind. We see a backyard born from our hearts...and lots of hard but enjoyable work. 🌿

Native stones help ponds blend seamlessly into the Hamanns' yard (above and left). Eye-popping gardens surround the barn that John built.

HERE'S THE
plan

1. Forsythia hedge
2. Daylily
3. Hosta
4. Variegated Hakonechloa grass
5. Pond
6. Star magnolia
7. Witch hazel
8. Dogwood
9. Rhododendron
10. Pink wisteria
11. Blue rose-of-Sharon
12. Silver grass
13. Lamium
14. Hydrangea
15. Weeping spruce
16. Perennials
17. Weeping pussy willow
18. Climbing euonymus
19. Apple tree
20. Maple
21. Weeping cedar
22. Locust tree
23. Mini bearded iris

$

BUDGET SECRET: Kathy Bomey of Duluth, Minnesota paid careful attention when landscapers installed a 700-gallon water garden in her front yard. When she decided to build a smaller pond in back, she was able to do it herself.

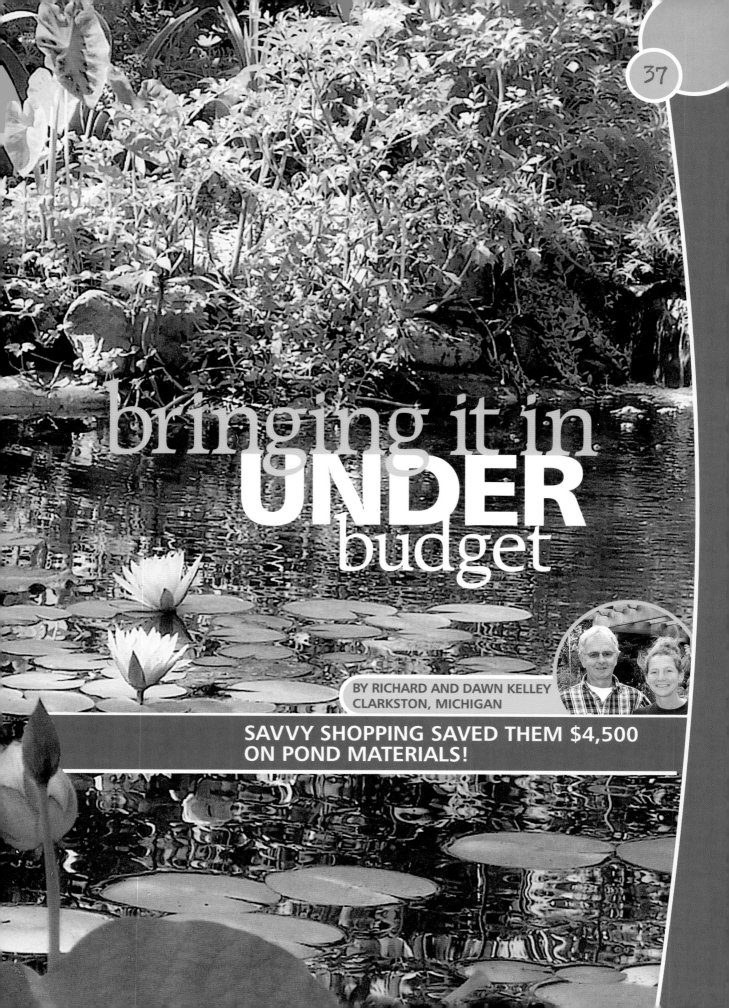

bringing it in UNDER budget

BY RICHARD AND DAWN KELLEY
CLARKSTON, MICHIGAN

SAVVY SHOPPING SAVED THEM $4,500 ON POND MATERIALS!

"Our pond was **10 years** in the making, but every minute was **worth it**."

When the pond was finished, Richard built a pergola, creating a pleasant spot for entertaining.

BUDGET SECRETS: 💲

Don't waste your money buying frogs. They'll find the pond as soon as you fill it!

To clean the water, use a pond filter with brushes instead of a pad. These filters cost a little more, but you don't have to replace them as often.

Think small. Full-grown koi are expensive, but the little fingerlings are only a few dollars each.

When I stand on our patio after a busy day, the mere sight of our tranquil pond provides instant relaxation. I'll never tire of hearing gurgling water or croaking frogs at dusk, or the sight of the riot of flowers surrounding it. But our yard wasn't always like this.

A decade earlier, there was nothing notable about it. It was just an overly shady space with too many mature trees and a patchwork of barely surviving grass. My husband, Richard, and I were gardening greenhorns, but we had to do something about the lawn. That's all it took to get us hooked on landscaping.

It took several years to work up the courage to start digging our backyard pond, though. We started small, installing a simple pond in one corner of the yard. Then we found more pond supplies at a clearance sale and added another. We were hooked. Several ponds later, we were ready for a major undertaking.

The only thing standing in our way was money. We learned supplies for one big pond could cost as much as $6,000!

I was accustomed to landscaping on a budget, and I knew I could do it again. I started by examining pond liners and pump kits at garden

(before)

(in progress)

centers. I discovered reliable brands for each, then searched the Internet for the same items and found them at a fraction of the cost. I was able to buy everything we needed for less than $1,500. It was a delightful experience!

BUDGET SECRET: Shop around, both electronically and at local stores, to find the best deal on supplies. If you want to splurge, spend it on a thick, rubberized pond liner. It should last a long time, and sharp rocks won't rip it.

$

39

Richard hand-shoveled a 30- by 35-foot terraced hole ranging in depth from 3 to 5 feet. The hard-packed clay soil was littered with stones, and Richard sometimes had to use a pickax to loosen the dirt before he could get a shovel into it. But we were able to save the stones for landscaping around the pond!

To make the pond look natural, I surrounded it with perennials, knowing they'd spread later. To save money, I bought plants at the end of the season. Some of the blooms were spent, but the prices were so low it didn't matter, and the flowers came back the next year.

Our pond was 10 years in the making, but every minute was worth it. We may build another, but I'm not sure we could top this! 🌿

HERE'S THE
plan

1. **SHADE GARDEN**
   Astilbe
   Bleeding heart
   Jacob's ladder
   Lily-of-the-valley

2. **WATER GARDEN**
   Corkscrew rush
   Elephant's ear
   Lotus
   Pennywort

3. **PERENNIAL BED**
   Purple coneflower
   Iris
   Ornamental grasses
   Russian sage

4. **ROSE GARDEN**
   'Carefree Delight'
   'Fourth of July'
   'Midas Touch'
   'Nancy Reagan'
   'Princess Diana'

5. **VEGETABLE GARDEN**
   Beans
   Cilantro
   Garlic
   Horseradish
   Lettuce
   Onions
   Parsley
   Rosemary
   Tomatoes

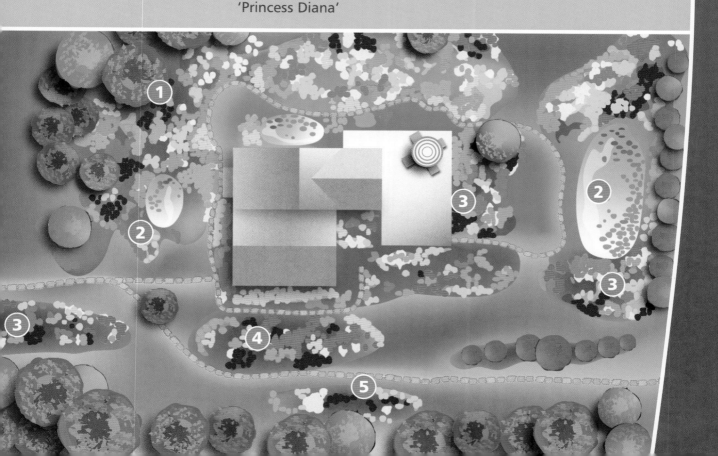

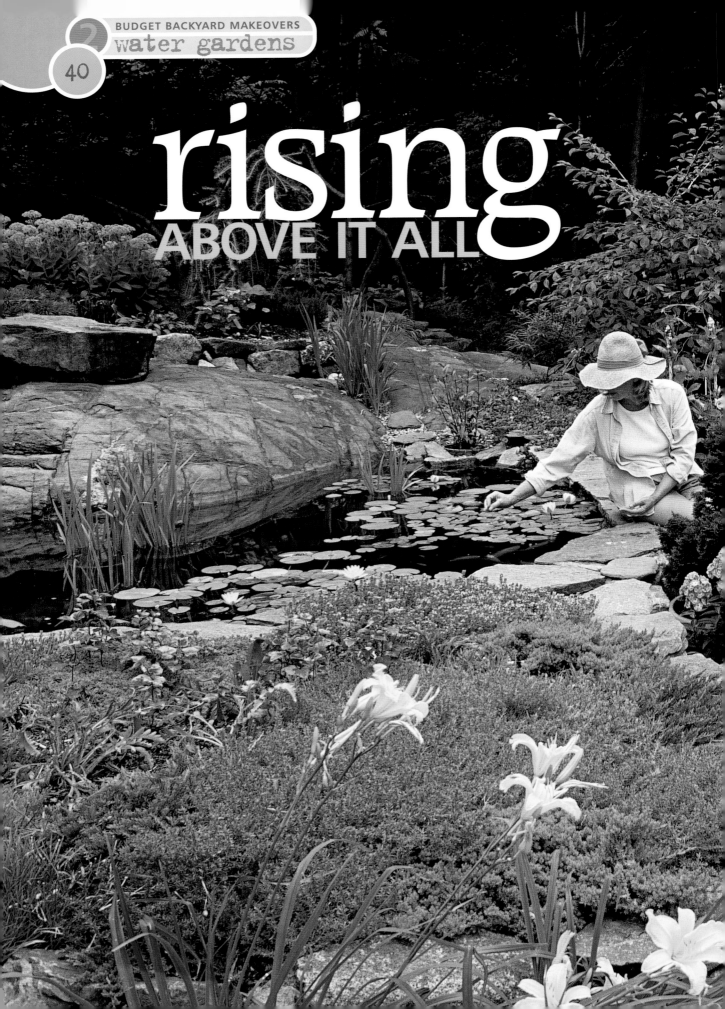

rising
ABOVE IT ALL

HER CREATIVE VISION TRANSFORMED A HARD-TO-TAME WOODLAND INTO A MASTERPIECE.

BETH GRADER
MARBLEHEAD, MASSACHUSETTS

BY TERI DUNN, GLOUCESTER, MASSACHUSETTS

Take a stroll with Beth Grader through her enchanting garden, and it's easy to think it's always been this way. She's not a fussy gardener, so her many trees and shrubs look more natural than highly manicured.

And that suits the birds, the bees, and Beth's little dog, "Tucker," just fine. The dog dashes past us and climbs the shade-dappled hillside, settling in a sandy spot that Beth calls "Tucker's Beach."

From that spot, you get a panoramic view of this impressive backyard in Marblehead, Massachusetts. It's bounded by a meandering stone wall and the sort of woods New Englanders are used to seeing—deciduous trees and their saplings, tangled undergrowth, and rocks everywhere, some half-hidden in the leaf litter. That's when Beth astonished me.

"The entire yard once looked like that," she said.

STARTING FROM SCRATCH

Beth and her husband, Buck, bought the undeveloped property in 1993. The location was perfect, backing up against conservation land. Buck, a builder by trade, began designing and overseeing construction of his family's new home. The garden was Beth's domain. All she needed to do was tame 1¼ wild acres.

In short order, the work crew pouring the foundation discovered the hill was mostly rock, or "ledge," as New Englanders call it. Beth wandered out into the "yard" wondering what to do…and where to begin.

She decided to start on high ground, an area opposite her future kitchen window, an

important spot for any gardener.

"Armed with a shovel, rake and hose, I just wandered out and started digging," Beth says. For months, she spent every spare moment digging down against an exposed piece of ledge.

Whenever anyone asked what she was doing, Beth replied, "Making a pond!"

Preformed liners for water gardens were not yet in vogue, and there was little written material or practical help for her ambitious idea. Buck eventually poured a concrete wall to hold back the earth on three sides. Then they had to paint everything with pool sealer and find ways to hide the pipes.

"Nobody would ever do it this way nowadays," Beth says, pausing to admire her mean-

dering koi, blooming water lilies and a browsing dragonfly. "Sometimes raccoons stop by, but the pool is deep enough that the fish can hide. So I don't mind."

A DETERMINED OUTLOOK

The completed pond fueled Beth's desire to create a spectacular yard. Nothing was going to stand in her way, but first she had to have numerous trees removed and large rocks rearranged.

She couldn't have a garden, or even a lawn, until truckloads of loam and compost were brought in. In a sense, her entire garden is one great raised bed, bounded by rocks and occasional reinforcing railroad ties.

A dozen years later, Beth's dogged determination is evident in the diverse plants and small trees that have grown to substantial size. Unusual choices include a gorgeous dawn redwood just past the hemlock hedge, and a dove tree off her deck.

Beth has shifted some shrubs around and adds new perennials and different herbs each year, so the scene is ever-changing.

Her perennials include a wide array of interesting cultivars you don't always see, and the organic vegetable garden sports unique varieties

Beth created a sense of seclusion in her garden with "double screening"—a double row of plants along every boundary. Taller plants in back and shorter ones in front create a natural "stepping-down" feel from the woods around the yard.

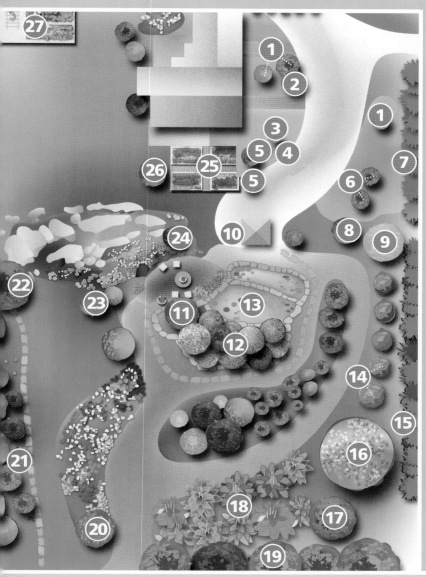

1. Japanese maple
2. Sweetbush
3. Lilac
4. Japanese snowball
5. Inkberry holly
6. Serviceberry
7. Hemlock hedge
8. Kousa dogwood
9. Dawn redwood
10. Goldflame honeysuckle
11. Stewartia tree
12. Conifer grove
13. Pond
14. Rhododendron
15. Yew hedge
16. Japanese cedar
17. Viburnum
18. Giant hosta
19. Ninebark hedge
20. Amur cork tree
21. Woodland
22. Oak
23. Carolina allspice
24. Crabapple
25. Herb garden
26. Dove tree
27. Vegetable garden

"Armed with a **shovel, rake** and **hose**, I just wandered out and started digging..."

of tomatoes, lettuces and beets.

Beth claims she never had an overall plan for the hilltop garden. Rolling up her sleeves was the only rule. And her personal interest in researching and trying new plants hasn't hurt, either.

To give her hilltop sanctuary a sense of seclusion, she uses "double screening," planting not one but two rows of plants along boundaries.

Beth suggests planting evergreens first, large or sprawling shrubs in front of those.

Under Beth's stewardship, the land has come alive. As she watches a hummingbird career around the blooming bounty in her garden, she muses, "This is a garden of discovery." Not only for the creatures that find sanctuary within its comfortable, beautiful boundaries, but for the gardener who created them. 🍃

GOT LEMONS?
make lemonade

THIS PAIR TURNED BACKYARD MISHAPS INTO GOLDEN OPPORTUNITIES.

A simple mistake can spur unexpected surprises. That's what you'll find when you step around back at Jim and Sharyn Richart's place in Hacienda Heights, California. Over the years, their backyard has been transformed from ho-hum to fabulous. And it all started when their son Jason accidentally left a garden hose running.

In most backyards, that would be an oversight. For the Richarts, who live high in the hills overlooking Los Angeles, it was a near catastrophe.

"A wall on our backyard hill slid down the slope," Jim explains. With the wall gone, it seemed like a good time to spruce up the yard.

**JIM AND SHARYN RICHART
HACIENDA HEIGHTS, CALIFORNIA**

Since that day, working in the backyard has been one of Jim's favorite escapes from the hectic pace of Southern California life.

"I've always had an interest in gardening and landscaping," he says. "This backyard has been a work in progress for the last 30 years. It's therapy...and when you're done, you see results."

Jim filled in the area where the wall once stood with a truckload of soil, widening the yard by 15 feet. "It gave us more usable space in the backyard," he says.

The missing wall was replaced with railroad ties buried 3 feet on end to outline the garden beds. Meanwhile, Sharyn added a vegetable garden and lots of containers.

Jim rigged up a drip irrigation system for

the containers, which allows the couple to leave home for weeks without worrying about the plants.

> # "It's therapy...and when you're done, you see results."

"It's all automatic," Jim says. "Without it, I'd have to work 8 hours a day just watering the plants."

Years later, a wildfire threatened their property. This time, a garden hose was Jim's friend. He used it to save the landscape and house by fighting smaller fires creeping down the hillside. "We were lucky," he says.

But the entire slope overlooking the backyard, with the exception of a few larger oak trees, needed to be replanted.

Again, Jim made the best of a bad situation. He selected drought-resistant plants, such as eucalyptus and sweetgum trees, and added irrigation to keep the hillside green all year.

Jim and Sharyn still felt something was missing. So they hired a contractor to help build a block retaining wall and stairway leading to a "garden center" that Jim built. It's the perfect place to start plants and do other behind-the-scenes chores.

"You get what you pay for," Jim recalls. "I had to work with the guy the whole time because we were playing catch-up...I ended up doing

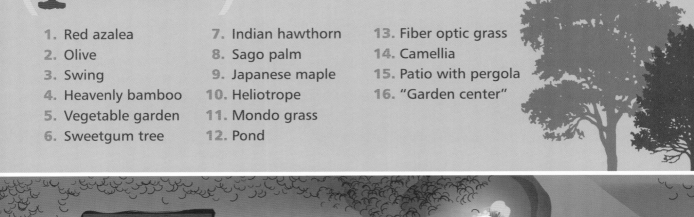

HERE'S THE plan

1. Red azalea
2. Olive
3. Swing
4. Heavenly bamboo
5. Vegetable garden
6. Sweetgum tree
7. Indian hawthorn
8. Sago palm
9. Japanese maple
10. Heliotrope
11. Mondo grass
12. Pond
13. Fiber optic grass
14. Camellia
15. Patio with pergola
16. "Garden center"

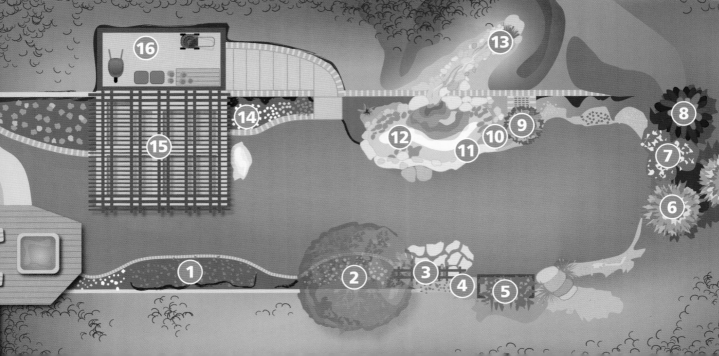

Doing your homework pays off. After months of research, Jim built his own pond in just 6 days. The revamped backyard is now his favorite place to unwind.

$ BUDGET SECRET: Jim saved thousands by installing the pond himself, and incorporated one feature—a bottom drain—that contractors wouldn't even consider. "I had bids from $6,900 to $16,000 to build a pond, none with a bottom drain," he says. "I did it a lot cheaper myself and added a ton of stuff, including the drain, which allows me to quickly control the water level during heavy rains."

most of the grunt work on the project."

From this experience, Jim decided that the crown jewel of the backyard—a natural-looking pond and waterfall—was too important of a project to trust to anyone else.

RESEARCH PAYS OFF

"This time, to build it right, I did it myself," Jim says. "I did a ton of research on the Internet, called pond suppliers, read 15 to 20 books and went on local pond tours to talk with owners. I learned a lot from other people's mistakes."

He installed a bottom drain in the pond, something no contractor would even consider because of the expense.

"I had bids from $6,900 to $16,000 to build a pond, none with a bottom drain," Jim says. "I did it cheaper myself and added a ton of stuff, including the drain, which allows me to quickly control the water level during heavy rains."

With the help of a few college students, Jim moved 13 tons of rock lining the 10- by 23-

foot water garden and waterfall. He completed the project in just 6 days!

"The waterfall was fairly easy to build," Jim explains. "There was a natural deer path leading into our yard down the hill, so I just dug a trench down the path because I knew that's where the water would naturally flow."

Jim and Sharyn love relaxing on the swing he built across from the pond, and Jim is trying to figure out how to add more color to the hillside. He's sure to find a way—even without a disaster to get him started. ❧

TAKING THE
plunge

KATHY DAUGHERTY
OWENSBORO, KENTUCKY

FILLING IN A POOL LET THEM CREATE THE YARD OF THEIR DREAMS.

Kathy and Andy agreed the focal point of their backyard would be a gazebo overlooking ponds and a waterfall.

BUDGET SECRETS:

Save money by building your own biological pond filter. Andy saved at least $400 this way, using a 100-gallon Rubbermaid tub and instructions he found on the Internet.

$

After digging a pond, use the extra soil to create flower beds. Susan Fisher of Attica, Indiana surrounded her pond with flagstone paths, then used the excess soil to make raised beds around the walkways.

BY BONNIE NANCE, OWENSBORO, KENTUCKY

One afternoon, Kathy Daugherty looked out the sliding glass doors to her backyard in Owensboro, Kentucky and made up her mind. The swimming pool had to go.

She and her husband, Andy, would be empty nesters in a couple of years, and no one was using the pool much anyway. Both were experiencing health problems, so they didn't need never-ending pool chores. What they needed was a place to relax.

After talking it over, Kathy and Andy decided to fill in the pool and create a landscape they could enjoy year-round. But first they had to decide what that landscape would include.

MORE ELBOW ROOM

Kathy, an avid gardener, had already covered every inch of available space with plants. Without a pool taking up most of the backyard, she'd have even more room to grow the flowers she loved.

As for Andy, he'd fantasized about a pond with fish and a peaceful waterfall. They'd never had enough space for that before. Without the pool, the possibilities were endless.

Kathy and Andy agreed the focal point would be a gazebo. Stone paths through the garden would make it a joy to stroll and would

(in progress)

simplify maintenance by providing easy access to the plants.

As their plans came together, the Daughertys couldn't wait to have a quiet place where they could relax and reflect, enjoying the birds, butterflies and hummingbirds their new plants would attract.

But first, they had a lot of work to do.

A contractor hauled in tons of dirt to fill in the swimming pool. The Daughertys did some research and learned proper drainage would be critical, so they hired an expert to take care of that part of the plan. Then the fun began.

BEEFING UP THE SOIL

Kathy knew it was vital to amend the heavy clay soil that now filled the backyard, so she worked in lots of compost. Mowing grass was never a chore she or Andy enjoyed, so they killed off the lawn with Roundup.

"I'd rather have flowers any day," Kathy says.

Andy then found a ready-made gazebo. They placed it in the center of the backyard and moved on to plans to put the pond around it.

Before he started digging, Andy read everything he could find on pond construction. He learned how to build a pond, and how to achieve the proper balance of water, plants and fish. Andy used a 100-gallon Rubbermaid tub and instructions he found on the Internet for a do-it-yourself biological pond filter, and

HERE'S THE plan

1. Peony
2. Hollyhock
3. Daylily
4. Larkspur
5. Coreopsis
6. Russian sage
7. Elephant's ear
8. Pine tree
9. Veronica
10. Sedum
11. Plumbago
12. Yarrow
13. Primrose
14. False indigo
15. Anemone
16. Bee balm
17. Coralbells
18. Hosta
19. Crabapple
20. Black-eyed Susan
21. Lavender
22. Shasta daisy
23. Stokes' aster

Flowers, stone paths and water gardens replaced the pool—and the grass—in the Daughtertys' yard.

saved at least $400, he says.

When he was finished, Andy had more than your typical water garden. It took 1,800 gallons to fill the three separate pools. One includes a waterfall built from carefully selected stones; another is filled with about 60 fish.

Although koi are a popular choice for water gardens, Andy prefers comets, common goldfish, fantails, orandas and shubunkins.

"I avoid koi or wakins (Japanese goldfish) because they eat too many plants that help keep the pond in balance," he says.

Gardening friends helped Kathy place the foundation plants. She added a dogwood for spring color, then moved on to butterfly bushes, daylilies, elephant's ears and roses.

"The key to continuous color is using a variety of plants—perennials, annuals, bulbs and herbs," Kathy says.

Kathy and Andy now spend more time than ever in their backyard. And neither of them misses having a lawn…or a swimming pool. 🌿

dirt
CHEAP

ARLENE AND ARLAN MARTIN
EAST EARL, PENNSYLVANIA

ARLENE AND ARLAN MARTIN
EAST EARL, PENNSYLVANIA

SHE GOT REMARKABLE RESULTS ON A SHOESTRING BUDGET.

The water gardens and flower beds in Arlene Martin's backyard look like a million bucks, but she didn't have to win a lottery to pay for them.

Thanks to resourcefulness, good luck and hard work, the breathtaking gardens at her home in East Earl, Pennsylvania cost around $200—and most of that went toward a water pump and filter.

"People are pretty shocked when they hear I only spent about $200," Arlene says. "I'm amazed by it myself, especially when I hear what other people spend on landscaping."

Two things inspired this budget-conscious landscaping project—special memories of New York's Finger Lakes region and a family room addition to Arlene's home.

"While living on my parents' farm in the Finger Lakes area, I fell in love with waterfalls and lakes," Arlene explains. "I missed them a lot when I moved to Pennsylvania.

"So when my husband, Arlan, and I added a window-filled family room onto our home, I thought a water garden would complement it perfectly. I figured we'd be able to enjoy it from inside the house as well as outside."

Arlan was excited, too, knowing it would mean less grass to cut, and more flowers that would attract birds and butterflies. But hiring a contractor to install a water garden would cost big bucks. Arlene decided to do it herself.

"I knew a pond liner would be very expensive," she says. "I got around that by salvaging an old vinyl swimming pool liner my sister was going to throw out.

"We also needed lots of stones to cover the liner edges and build a waterfall. But instead of buying them, we gathered rocks from my parents' farm. Arlan and our sons, Austin

and Addison, helped collect stones every time we visited."

The hardest part was digging up the yard for the ponds. Arlene built the lower pond one year and the upper pond the next, using just a hand shovel. She learned all she needed to know by reading books on ponds.

Most of her plants were gifts from family and friends, so that saved money, too.

"One friend gave me 100 tulip bulbs," Arlene says. "Every time a flower blooms, I think of the person who gave it to me."

To cut costs even further, she starts many flowers from seed.

"The perennials keep growing and growing, so we keep dividing them and either create more beds to hold them, or add on to the existing beds," Arlene says. "I'm always amazed at how fast perennials spread—that's what's so great about them. The more space they take up, the fewer annuals I have to plant. Plus, I enjoy dividing perennials and swapping with friends."

Would Arlene ever tackle such a big project again? You bet she would!

"It was worth all the work," she enthuses. "Our gardens attract lots of butterflies and bees, not to mention hummingbirds and dragonflies. And the birds enjoy bathing in and drinking from the water gardens.

"It's very relaxing to sit on our deck and listen to the music of the waterfall and the birds. We love it." ❦

HERE'S THE plan

1. Family room addition
2. Deck
3. Perennial beds
4. Maple
5. Pond
6. Waterfall
7. Ornamental grasses
8. Annual bed
9. Herb garden
10. White pine

BY DARLEEN AND DAVE GRANGER
CONCORD, MICHIGAN

THE TIDE THAT
binds

BUILDING A POND BROUGHT THIS FAMILY EVEN CLOSER.

When people see our hand-dug garden pond just off the back deck, they usually ask, "What was the hardest part of building it?"

Most of the time, they expect me to mention shoveling or rock-hauling. When I answer, "Just getting started," they genuinely look surprised. The hardest part was convincing everyone in our family that the time was right to "dig in."

I had to convince Dave, my cautious husband, not to worry…it would all come together just as we planned. And the kids are never hesitant about taking on projects.

We needed to finish this big one before Sarah, Mark and Kevin went off to college or began their careers. Our youngest, Faith, was 7 at the time, and a swimming hole just out the back door suited her fine. Once everyone was on board, there was no turning back.

GATHERING IDEAS

It didn't take long for us to decide what we wanted. We agreed a large pond near our back deck, at the bottom of the sloping hillside, would be a natural fit. For nearly 7 years, we collected ideas from magazines and books, keeping a file until we were ready to take the plunge.

Kevin, our youngest son, was only 16, but he was the project foreman. He has a God-given talent to visualize things and envision how to put them together. He suggested building a 16- by 18-foot pond, below the waterfalls of three smaller cascading ponds.

Kevin also installed a biofilter, a gravel-based natural filter that keeps the pond chemically balanced. It's buried in a mound near the upper pond. A small pump in the large pond keeps the water circulating.

DIGGING IN

We used garden hoses to lay out the shape of the ponds, then sprinkled flour over them to create an outline to dig around.

Even with all six of us pitching in, it took several days to dig the entire pond with hand shovels. We used one wheelbarrow and a small garden tractor with a trailer to haul the excavated soil, piling most of it around the ponds to

keep runoff from entering the water.

The deepest part of the pond is 3-1/2 feet, so goldfish and frogs can winter there. The front edge near the deck is only 6 inches deep. Along the sides, we built shelves about 18 inches deep for potted water plants.

This project was even more fun than I even billed it to be…until a mudslide washed away most of the work we'd done. The kids' perseverance was amazing. They seemed to thrive on challenges like this.

Once the digging was complete, we covered the ponds with a large, old swimming pool liner as a pad for the actual pond liners, leaving lots of excess around the edges so we could make adjustments as we added water.

The pond cost about $2,000. But it's worth a lot more than that in sentimental value.

We enjoy its soothing effect, and it's provided a beautiful backdrop as I've home-schooled our kids. We've become very close, and I'm glad we have this special place to relax and talk on warm evenings.

We've worked on many projects over the years, but this one has been our most "splashing success." ❦

HERE'S THE
plan

1. Daffodil
2. Bleeding heart
3. Hosta
4. Tulip
5. Iris
6. Peony
7. Periwinkle
8. Lake Superior driftwood and rocks
9. 'Pacific Sunset' hybrid maple
10. Beardtongue
11. Swing
12. Oriental lily
13. Flowering almond
14. Dogwood
15. Flowering crabapple
16. Lilac
17. Yucca
18. Purple coneflower
19. Flowering cherry

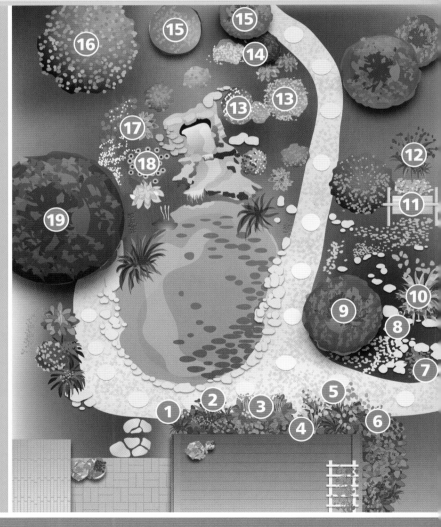

$

BUDGET SECRET: Double-pad it. The Grangers put an old swimming pool liner beneath the pond liners to protect them from sharp rocks and other objects that may create leaks.

HE STRUCK water!

OVER THE LAST 15 YEARS, TOM CLARK TURNED A "MUD HOLE" INTO THIS SPLASHING SUCCESS.

BY TOM CLARK, YORK, MAINE

Back in 1991, when my wife and I moved to this property in York, Maine, the first thing I purchased was a beat-up backhoe. It came in handy for digging up the stumps dotting our landscape.

After removing several, I dug a large hole to bury them. To my surprise, I tapped into a natural spring that immediately filled the hole. It looked like we were going to have a pond!

I started with a small sump pump to remove water as I moved large boulders from our property to the "mud hole."

Trying to place large rocks in a very deep hole isn't easy, and even harder with a very tired and worn-out backhoe. Many times, I'd try to place a rock just so, only to knock it down when adding the next. It took me several months to finish, and within 6 months, the main wall fell!

It was back to rebuilding. Because I enjoyed cooling off in the pond, I decided to expand it, despite my wife's objections. She thought I was spending too much time below ground level, and the rock work was taking a toll on my aging body.

I added a waterfall, requiring a smaller pond above the original. Through trial and error, I learned preformed ponds wouldn't work. I went to pond liners. What a difference...you can make these any size and easily build waterfalls!

Since I was getting the hang of it, I decided to redo the main pond walls to make them look more formal. In the process, I accidentally knocked down the main wall. This setback was huge. The collapse nearly killed the project.

I'm glad it didn't. I spent hundreds of additional hours adding more ponds and waterfalls and cleaning up messy rock work. In my 10th year, two things finally happened. I added fish and got my first compliment. "Starting to look pretty good!" someone said. That was motivating and has kept me going! 🌿

BUDGET SECRETS:

$

"Save square rocks for the face of walls. I wasted many good rocks, putting them in areas that you can't see."

"Avoid buying a replacement pond liner by placing a soft, sandy bed below your liner first. I learned the hard way by ripping my liner after building a wall on top of it."

budget project #2

build this fountain
IN AN AFTERNOON

YES, YOU CAN AFFORD A BACKYARD FOUNTAIN!

BY GREGG CARLSEN
STILLWATER, MINNESOTA

This quaint fountain is proof that good things come in small packages. I was able to build mine in an afternoon for about $75. With more expensive rocks, you might spend $125 at most—still a bargain.

This is a "disappearing fountain," so there's no exposed standing water. This means there's less maintenance, since there's less chance debris and critters will wind up in the water.

Yet it provides the soothing sight and sound of running water people love. Another bonus—since birds love moving water, there's a chance you'll attract some of these outdoor friends.

You can personalize your fountain in a number of ways:

- Surround it with any type of rock. I used a natural wall stone, but you can use modular concrete retaining-wall blocks, boulders or flagstone.
- Top it off with any type of small stone. I used a decorative rock called "Western Sunset." You can use pebbles, lava stone or even special rocks you've collected in your travels.
- Use any bowl, dish or plate you want for the water to splash into. I opted for three pieces, so the water cascades from one dish into the next.

GETTING STARTED

I used a whiskey barrel liner from the local home center for the catch basin, but any large plastic container will do (see Photo 1 on page 58). Some garden centers sell special pond liners just for this purpose.

Regardless of your soil conditions, nestle your catch basin or liner in a bed of sand. This helps protect the bottom of the tub from sharp rocks, and makes it easier to level the tub and the first course of rock.

I constructed my fountain so I could gain

HOW IT ALL GOES TOGETHER

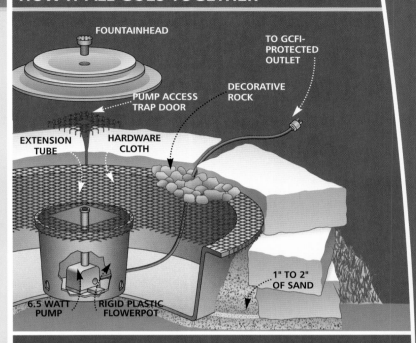

FOUNTAINHEAD

TO GCFI-PROTECTED OUTLET

PUMP ACCESS TRAP DOOR

DECORATIVE ROCK

EXTENSION TUBE

HARDWARE CLOTH

1" TO 2" OF SAND

6.5 WATT PUMP

RIGID PLASTIC FLOWERPOT

FOUR FOUNTAINHEADS, FOUR COOL LOOKS

All four of these interchangeable fountainheads (below), which provide different looks, came in one package. It took part of an afternoon to build this fountain, and it didn't take any fancy tools.

access to the pump by removing a handful of rocks along with the hardware cloth trap door (Photo 5). This allows us to easily remove the pump for maintenance and for storing it indoors over the winter.

Use a bag of sand as a workbench when drilling the holes in your bowls and dishes (Photo 6). It'll provide a cushion and help prevent breakage.

Many large garden centers and home centers sell water garden pumps and accessories. Or you can contact:

- **Laguna,** *www.lagunaponds.com*
- **Little Giant Pump Co.**
  1-888/956-0000
  www.lgpc.com
- **MacArthur Water Gardens**
  1-800/695-4913
  www.macarthurwatergardens.com

fountain project

STEPS	ONE:	TWO:	THREE:	FOUR:
	SELECT A LOCATION	PICK OUT A FLOWERPOT	MAKE ROOM FOR THE PUMP	DRESS UP THE PERIMETER

Select a location where you'll enjoy your fountain, hollow out a 2-inch-deep area, then level in a bed of sand large enough to accommodate the plastic tub and the rock or block that will surround it.

Locate a sturdy plastic flowerpot the same height as your plastic tub, cut a hole in the side near the bottom, and feed the cord for the electric pump through it. Position this pot right side up in the center of your tub.

BUDGET SECRET:

Don't waste money on a fancy fountain dish. Instead, showcase something from your kitchen that you rarely use but just can't bear to throw out. You can use a plate, saucer, bowl...even a teapot!

Cut a small piece of hardware cloth a few inches larger than the access hole to create a removable trap door, then cut a small opening for the pump stem. Cover the top of the hardware cloth with decorative stone.

⚠️ **OPERATING TIPS:** Keep your fountain liner full of water and check the level every day or so, especially in hot weather. Use any thin stick as a dipstick to check the water level.

- Plug your pump into a GFCI-protected outlet—ideally one located next to the fountain. If you use an extension cord, leave it exposed so you know where it is, and be careful with sharp garden tools and mowers.

- As a precaution, unplug the fountain when you're not around to watch it (or put it on a timer). If the pump runs dry, it'll burn out.

- Most pumps will accept a variety of fountainheads. Bear in mind that with some spray patterns, all the water may not drain back into the tub. With this type of fountain, you'll have to refill your tub much more often.

FIVE:	**SIX:**	**SEVEN:**
MAKE A TRAP DOOR	DRILL THE FOUNTAIN DISH	INSTALL, PLUG IN...RELAX!

PUMP ACCESS OPENING

Cut a hole in the wire hardware cloth (available at home centers) large enough for the pump to fit through, then position the cloth over the tub and bend the edges over the tub lip.

Surround the tub with flagstone or concrete retaining-wall blocks to match the rest of your landscape. The upper course should be about 2 inches higher than the top of the tub.

CERAMIC TILE BIT

BAG OF SAND

Drill a hole in your fountain dish by first scoring the glaze in the center of the bowl with a light tap of a nail, then boring a hole using a ceramic tile bit. If you need to enlarge the hole, use a larger bit or small file.

Install the fountainhead of your choice. Most pumps can accommodate a range of heads, including mushroom-shaped, cup-shaped and fan-shaped patterns (see page 57). Then fill the tub, plug in the pump and relax.

BRIGHTideas

DIVING IN

Creating your own pond is an ambitious undertaking, but you needn't be a pro. Do your homework first, and the rewards will be sweet indeed.

builder's estimate: $25,000.
actual cost: $2,500.
doing it yourself: priceless.

Contractors told Don Spillner it would cost $25,000 to build the Japanese water garden he wanted for his Fort Wayne, Indiana backyard. So he did it himself. After digging a 3,000-gallon hole, Don salvaged building materials like rocks, pea gravel, sand and railroad ties. He also built the pond filter, footbridge and bamboo bench. Out-of-pocket costs: A mere $2,500—one-tenth what he would've paid a contractor.

taking center stage

When Joyce and Elmer Walters bought their farm 13 years ago, the sprawling yard was bare except for a stand of evergreens. "The space really called out for something dramatic," Joyce says. So she started digging—first by hand, then with a backhoe—to create this stunning pond, which she and Elmer surrounded with plants and seating areas. "It turned out to be the spectacular centerpiece our yard needed," she says.

sticking with stones

Flagstone edges help this pond blend in with Louann Korzan's backyard in Stratford, Oklahoma. Louann began building backyard features with rocks after watching builders put artificial-stone facing on her chimney. Her tip: Use only rocks that are small and easy to lift. "It takes more time and patience, but it's definitely worth the trouble," Louann says.

for the birds

Larry O'Neal designed this two-level pool in Rockford, Illinois with birds in mind. The upper pool has shallow water where birds can bathe and drink, then cascades into a larger pond. "It's become the centerpiece of our backyard," Larry says. The birds like it, too—Larry and his wife, Betty, have spotted dozens of species drinking and bathing there.

PLANTS TO KEEP PONDS
HEALTHY & BEAUTIFUL

'red flare'

waterlilies

These stars of the water garden provide a floating carpet of leaves and flowers, casting shade for fish and depriving algae of sunlight. Hardy types bloom summer through fall. During cold weather, the foliage dies and sinks. New leaves rise from the submerged rhizomes in spring. In colder regions, tropical types are usually treated as annuals or overwintered indoors. These produce fragrant white, yellow, pink, red or lilac flowers and are available in day- or night-blooming varieties. The five types listed here need full sun.

TOP PICKS

'Pink Sensation': This hardy lily stays open later in the day than any other pink. Its flower size ranges from 5 to 6 inches.

'Colorado': This hardy bloomer has salmon flowers with lighter tips. Blooms are 4 to 5 inches across.

'Laydekeri Fulgens': Good for any size pond, this hardy lily has 5- to 6-inch crimson flowers that are first to appear in spring and last into fall.

'Red Flare': This tropical lily blooms in the evening, with big (7- to 10-inch) deep-red flowers and dark bronze leaves.

'Green Smoke': A tropical day-bloomer, its 5- to 6-inch flowers are an interesting mix of yellows, greens and blues.

marginal plants

Generally taller plants, marginals grow on the water's edge, add shade and smooth the transition from the pond to the plants surrounding it. Marginals need 1 to 8 inches of water and may be tropical or hardy. Stack stones around them to camouflage the pots. Move tropical plants, pots and all, indoors for winter.

TOP PICKS

Sweet flag: Features stiff, shiny green straplike leaves 2 to 4 feet tall. Needs full to partial sun.

Blue flag iris: A showy midseason bloomer, it boasts blue-violet flowers and sword-like leaves 2 to 3 feet tall. Needs full sun to partial shade.

Miniature cattail: Small brown seed heads rise above slender, stiff leaves in late summer; 18 to 24 inches tall. Needs full to partial sun.

'Tropicana' canna: A tropical stunner with striped leaves that change from burgundy to red, pink, yellow and gold. The center vein remains chartreuse. Flowers are orange. Three to 4 feet tall. Needs full sun.

Water hyssop: This tropical has tiny oval leaves and delicate white blossoms that persist all summer. Needs full sun.

'tropicana' canna

AQUATIC PLANTS SHADE AND SHELTER YOUR FISH, ATTRACT SONGBIRDS AND FROGS, AND KEEP THE WATER HEALTHY BY OXYGENATING IT AND INHIBITING ALGAE GROWTH. AND THEY LOOK BEAUTIFUL, TOO.

floating plants

Floating foliage shades the water and absorbs excess nutrients, inhibiting algae growth. Most floaters are tropical plants. In colder climates, treat tropical types as annuals or overwinter them indoors.

TOP PICK

Water lettuce: Velvety blue-green ribbed leaves form a rosette. Roots offer shelter for fish. Plant with care—it's banned in some states. Needs full to partial sun.

water lettuce

submerged plants

Often overlooked because they aren't readily visible, these hardy plants keep algae in check, oxygenate the water, and provide cover for small fish and frogs. To plant, just push a bundle of plants into the gravel at the bottom of the pond–that's it!

TOP PICKS

Hornwort: Resembles a spruce tree; branchy stems provide habitat for spawning fish. Needs full to partial sun.

Fanwort: Although it grows at pond's bottom, its white flowers and cheery foliage are sometimes visible at the surface. Needs full to partial sun.

lotuses

These aquatic beauties are noted for their magnificently fragrant flowers and round leaves. The attractive seedpods are often used in dried-flower arrangements. Lotus plants are aggressive; keep them in pots to prevent them from spreading. These three types need full to partial sun.

TOP PICKS

'Mrs. Perry D. Slocum': Nine- to 12-inch blooms are pink flushed with yellow the first day, changing to pink and yellow the second and, finally, cream and pink the third. Strong anise fragrance.

'Momo Botan': Perfect for small ponds and tub gardens, its double blooms are rose-pink. Rich, spicy scent.–

'Shiroman': Features double snowy-white blooms up to 12 inches across.

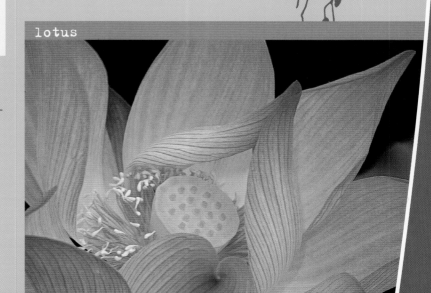

lotus

from the
ground up

③

FROM RAGS
to riches

BY BERNIE AND MARY ECKERT
HAMBURG, NEW YORK

THIS SEASONED LANDSCAPER'S FIVE-STEP APPROACH TURNED AN EMPTY YARD INTO A VIBRANT SHOWSTOPPER.

After 3 decades of landscaping experience, I knew one thing for sure when my wife, Mary, and I moved into our mobile home in Hamburg, New York in the late 1980s—the yard needed some major improvements.

From first glance it seemed to be screaming, "Help!" All that surrounded our home was a small concrete patio and grass. That's it…no trees, no shrubs, no annuals or perennials.

At the time, we thought this would be our home for the rest of our lives, so I was determined to make my personal stamp on the property. For me to be happy, I had to have a balance of the five essential ingredients for continuous color—spring bulbs, perennials, annuals, and flowering trees and shrubs.

By using this mix of plants, we ended up with constant color, from the time the first crocus opened in spring until western New York's first killing frost did in our annuals in November. The best part? Each year, the show got bigger and better as the plants matured and produced even more abundant blooms.

My top priority was to build a patio and add some landscaping around it, creating what I call the "outdoor living area."

Curved lines bring lots of dimension to any landscape, so I arranged brick pavers in a circular pattern in a central part of the lawn.

As Mary developed arthritis, however, it became more difficult for her to walk in the yard. So I moved our patio closer to the back door, building two semicircles, again with paver bricks.

To do this, I removed and reused the bricks from inside the old round patio, leaving a narrow circular pathway around what eventually became another flower bed, the main focal point of the yard.

To surround the new patio with beauty, I built raised beds.

I created a natural edging with some of the 4-foot oak logs we had lying in the yard. I dug a 2-foot-deep trench and set the logs side-by-side on end before backfilling the soil to hold them in place.

Good planting soil is a must, so I loaded the raised beds with a mixture of topsoil, peat moss and sand.

Then I was ready for some fun—selecting the plants.

OVERLAPPING PLANTINGS

To achieve maximum color, I struck a balance by using plants from the five groups I mentioned earlier.

Spring bulbs are a necessity because they bring early color and set the tone for the growing season. For the best results, I plant them in groups of 20 or more bulbs, which creates a natural look that delivers a big splash of color.

As the spring bulbs complete their cycle, perennials begin to take over. The good thing about perennials is that you plant them once and they return year after year.

However, most perennials bloom for only a short period. That's why it's important to plant varieties that flower at different times. Some of my favorites are creeping phlox, summer phlox, alpine rock cress, coreopsis, gaillardia, Shasta daisy, astilbe, daylily and black-eyed Susan.

> "I was determined to leave my **personal stamp** on the property."

Since perennial color comes and goes, garden annuals are necessary for a prolonged show. I plant most of mine after the tulips, daffodils, hyacinths and crocus have faded.

I place them in the same areas as the spring flowers, thereby hiding the bulbs' wilting foliage (which feeds the plants for the next blooming season).

My favorite thing about annuals, however, is

that there are so many choices. No flower bed has to look the same from year to year.

A BEAUTIFUL BACKDROP

Flowering trees and shrubs create the background for my other plants. Just like perennials, these permanent plants bloom for short periods, so it's important to pick varieties that blossom at different intervals.

Because trees and shrubs require a far greater investment, and there's such a large selection to choose from, you'll want to give it lots of thought before making a purchase. I recommend going to a nursery several times during the year so you can see when trees and shrubs will add color to your landscape.

Some of my personal favorites are flowering dogwood, rhododendron, sand cherry, purple-leaf plum, spirea and hemlock.

Yes, this project was pretty ambitious. But by combining these five ingredients from the start, we basked in the beauty of vibrant flowers throughout the entire growing season. ❧

"No **flower bed** has to look the same from year to year."

Bernie relies on five essential ingredients to make sure something's always in bloom—spring bulbs, annuals, perennials, and flowering trees and shrubs.

SHED

HOUSE

1. Grapevine
2. Clematis
3. Climbing rose
4. Holly
5. Annuals and perennials
6. Purple-leaf plum
7. Azalea
8. Rhododendron
9. Dogwood
10. Gate
11. Daffodil
12. Sand cherry
13. Spirea
14. Bird feeder
15. Flowering quince
16. Hemlock

WELL-ROOTED IN
family

THIS COUPLE BUILT THEIR GARDEN WITH PLANTS FROM RELATIVES AND FRIENDS.

**RICK AND RHONDA SANBORN
KEZAR FALLS, MAINE**

Rhonda transplanted hemlocks to create a hedge, and built a waterfall with stones unearthed when her house was built (top). Family and friends provided most of the plants.

First-time visitors to Rhonda and Rick Sanborn's home might think they spent a small fortune creating their ever-blooming backyard. While their backyard is "rich" in plantings, it cost the Sanborns next to nothing.

Almost everything in their lovingly landscaped yard in Kezar Falls, on the southern coast of Maine, has been passed on from friends and relatives.

"Our gardens are filled with plants people gave us," Rhonda says. "We never bought a thing until just the last few years."

The hilltop property did not always look this lush. It was originally an apple orchard on a dairy farm owned by Rhonda's grandparents. When Rhonda received the land as a gift about 30 years ago, there was nothing on it but a few tree stumps.

BUDGET SECRET:
Use the natural resources around you to beautify the landscape. Rhonda used rocks unearthed during her home's excavation to build stone walls.

From the very beginning, Rhonda relied on the surrounding natural resources to beautify the landscape. When builders blasted out a rock ledge for the house's foundation, she used the leftover rubble to build the first of many stone walls—while carrying her infant daughter in a baby-carrier backpack.

"There were rocks everywhere, and I had to start putting them someplace," Rhonda laughs.

"Soon I was hooked on rocks. Every time I saw a flat rock somewhere, I'd bring it home. I knew nothing about rock-wall building. I just did it."

LOOKING FOR TRANSPLANTS

When she wasn't building walls, Rhonda was out in the surrounding woods, looking for trees and shrubs to transplant around the house.

"My dad owned lots of land, so I dug up lots of white birches. I lined one side of the yard with pines from his property," she says. "Then I transplanted some hemlocks and shaped them into hedges."

It wasn't long before Rhonda's friends and relatives recognized her passion for planting. New starts began arriving.

"I also started rescuing plants they wanted to discard—everything from lilacs to hostas, primroses to rosebushes, and all types of trees. Before long, my yard began to take on a personality all its own."

As the plants multiplied and spread, Rhonda divided and transplanted them into new garden beds. Cuttings from her grandmothers' roses have multiplied into more than 75 rosebushes, cascading over the full length of one rock wall and part of the picket fence surrounding the swimming pool.

"I treasure these links to the past," Rhonda says. "When you look at certain plants, it reminds you of where they came from."

After Rick and Rhonda married, Rick dug in and planted some family heirlooms of his own, including irises that came from England in the

Lush roses lend privacy to the pool area. Rhonda grew them from cuttings her grandmothers provided.

1800s, plus hostas and lilies from his friends and grandparents.

"In every open corner, Rick can see a garden," Rhonda says. "He has played a big part in what our backyard looks like today."

Rick convinced Rhonda to add a bed next to the stone wall at the back of the yard, where 300 tulips and daffodils bloom each spring. Bearded and Japanese irises bloom next, followed by bright Oriental lilies and airy cleomes and cosmos.

Rick also designed a new figure-eight garden,

where Rhonda built a pond and waterfall among the lilacs, cosmos, cleomes and dahlias.

Colorful hollyhocks, hibiscus, potentilla and clematis surround the swimming pool. There's also a spot there for the hosta garden Rick always wanted.

"He convinced me that we shouldn't cut down the pines that seemed to outgrow their space," Rhonda says. "Instead, we decided to trim the bottom branches and create a 100-foot shade garden for the hostas, and also lady's-slipper, columbine, jack-in-the-pulpit, ferns, ajuga

BUDGET SECRETS:

Save money by transplanting young trees yourself. Rhonda dug up most of her trees from property her father owned.

Create a "memory garden" with plants from friends and relatives. Rhonda's yard features more than 75 rosebushes—all started with cuttings from her grandmothers.

Rhonda taught herself how to build rock walls like this one. Dense flower beds flank the path to the pool (below).

$

"We never bought a thing until just the last couple of years."

and impatiens."

The Sanborns also installed a garden railroad in a bed of miniature perennials near one of their ponds. It delights their grandchildren, who seem to have inherited the family gardening genes.

"Each child has a special garden. We help them if they need it, but they pick the plants and do most of the work themselves," Rhonda says proudly. 🌿

1. Rose garden
2. Hosta garden
3. Hemlock hedge
4. Goldfish pond
5. Arbor
6. Gazebo
7. Fountain
8. Flowering crabapple

9. Perennial garden
10. Pond and waterfall
11. Climbing rose
12. Maple
13. Shade garden
14. Pine tree
15. Spring bulbs
16. Birch tree

$ BUDGET SECRET: If you need plants to fill new beds, let others know you'd welcome their garden castoffs. Rhonda "rescued" plants that friends are relatives wanted to discard—everything from hostas to trees. "Before long, my yard began to take on a personality all its own," she says.

the bigger, THE BETTER!

A BLANK CANVAS OF 2½ ACRES WAS JUST
WHAT THIS GARDENER WANTED.

BY JOYCE AND KEITH SMITTKAMP
DECATUR, ILLINOIS

For as long as I can remember, I've been a gardener. At 7, I was "planting" sticks and rocks around my favorite tree. Half a century later, I'm still planting.

We moved to our current home after I told my husband, Keith, we needed more space for perennials. I actually suggested he tear down the garage to make room.

Instead, he found this 2-1/2-acre yard where I could go wild. I started digging even before we moved in! One of the first things we had to do was build a small shed for my garden tools, about 200 feet from the house.

A SNEAK PEEK AT HEAVEN

The yard came with mature trees, a few ornamental bushes and lots of lawn. I told my daughter I wanted flowers growing from the shed to the house on both sides of the yard. It sounded unrealistic, but with endless hours of hard work, I made it happen. Now, when I look out the living room window, it's like sneaking a peek into Heaven!

I've made more than a dozen flower beds, taking time to amend the soil in each one before planting. I've hauled 20 tons of rock and gravel and four truckloads of black dirt, one wheelbarrow at a time. I've moved railroad ties, landscape timber and flagstone, and I've built pergolas, trellises, fences and birdhouses.

> "I've hauled 20 tons of rock and gravel and **four truck-loads** of black dirt, one wheelbarrow at a time."

Keith admires my enthusiasm and will help if I ask, but there's a certain satisfaction to saying, "I did it myself!"

A TRICKY CHALLENGE

The trickiest area to landscape was the east side of our house. Two downspouts and a sump pump drained into the small side yard. It was low, always wet, and had an unappealing view of the neighbor's garbage cans. This was the only practical route to our backyard from the front of the house, so it was high on my to-do list.

A privacy fence created a whole new look and spurred more ideas. I made an arched trellis to create a welcoming entryway and laid a gravel path, using old heat registers as stepping-stones. Since this area is shady and moist, I planted lots of hostas, created a small and relaxing Oriental garden, and added huge pots of impatiens.

Although annuals add color to my garden, perennials are my greatest love. I have several hundred varieties of perennials and am always looking for new ones. How can you not be impressed by plants that endure the most extreme Midwest weather and still come back more beautiful than ever?

Since there's so much to see in our yard, I created several seating areas to enjoy the

HERE'S THE
(plan)

1. Oriental garden
2. Arched trellis
3. Pond
4. Perennial garden
5. Hosta
6. Ornamental grasses
7. Bridge
8. Oak tree
9. Pergola
10. Red maple
11. Redbud
12. Split-rail fence
13. Shed
14. Tomato garden
15. Compost
16. Corncrib gazebo
17. Shade garden
18. Bald cypress
19. White pine
20. Sweetgum tree
21. Maple
22. Nature area
23. Fire pit
24. Locust tree
25. Tulip tree

HOUSE

edge of the pond, including water-loving ones like yellow moneywort, which trails over and between the rocks and into the water.

As I dug the pond, I piled the dirt right behind it for a raised bed. This area's very flat, so the raised bed makes the pond look larger than it is. Tall plants enhance this illusion. I also built a small bridge next to the pond and laid a flagstone patio around it.

RAISING THE BAR

An area beyond the pond needed a makeover, too. The previous owners had grown vegetables there for about 50 years. It was sunny, but low and damp, so I built a split-rail fence around it and added four raised beds. A

Joyce turned an old corncrib into a cozy gazebo (above) and furnished it with salvaged items, then built a pergola to support a hammock.

BUDGET SECRETS:

Old heat registers make charming and unusual stepping-stones for a gravel path.

Look for freebies. A tree-trimming service gives Joyce wood mulch at no charge.

view. One of my favorites is the "country gazebo" made from an old corncrib.

My daughter and son-in-law gave it to me for Christmas. (Yes, I asked for it!) It's a great place to relax--and economical, too. We furnished it with salvaged items and hand-me-downs, from the wicker furniture to the chandelier.

I also wanted a pond. To make it look as natural as possible, I surrounded it with a shallow ledge 6 inches deep and 10 inches wide. On this ledge, I placed stones and boulders so they're partially submerged. Plants come right up to the

tree-trimming service gives me wood mulch for free, so I used that to make paths around the beds.

To create more interest, I added a square trellis—four treated round posts anchored in concrete and strung with ropes. It's beautiful covered with sweet autumn clematis.

After completing that project, I wanted a place to relax! I made a pergola with benches and a hammock. After all, what good is all that work if you don't have a place to kick back and soak it all in? 🍃

A TOUCH OF
magic

THRIFT AND
CREATIVITY TRANSFORMED PILES OF
BARE DIRT INTO A JUNGLE PARADISE.

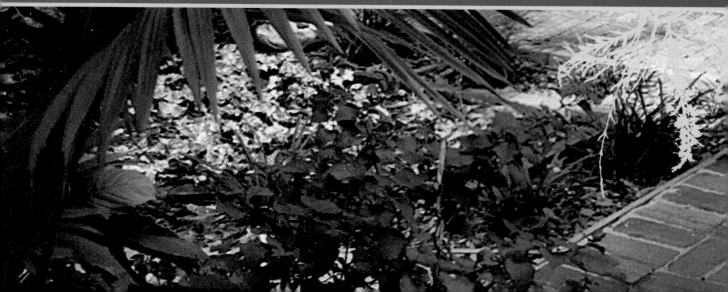

**BY COLLEEN AND RANDY BUSS
WINTER GARDEN, FLORIDA**

A little bit of that Disney magic has found its way into our backyard. That's because my creative husband, Randy, has turned all his efforts to our little paradise since retiring from the most popular theme park in Florida.

The results are jaw-dropping. In less than 2 years, he transformed our landscape from dirt mounds into a tropical jungle.

Randy spends all his time working in the backyard, stopping only to read the newspaper on the deck in the morning. After that, it's back to work—one project has led to another since we moved in about 4 years ago.

While I'm proud of the beauty we've brought to our small urban landscape, Randy is more proud that we accomplished all this for less than $750!

LET THERE BE LIGHT

We can't say our yard was created from a grand plan. But we had a few well-defined priorities. We didn't want a lawn to maintain, and I wanted a brick patio in front of our screened porch.

We also knew how important it was to bury water and electrical lines throughout the property before breaking ground. We took our best guess as to where the buried lines should emerge. Even if we were off by a few feet, we figured it would be easier to make adjustments rather than try to run the lines after the fact.

Randy built a wishing well to hide a water spigot and electrical outlet, and surrounded the patio with lush plants.

BUDGET SECRET: $

Before you move to a new home, divide and pot some of your favorite perennials at your old one. If the plants are a bit overgrown, you'll be doing the new owners a favor—but be sure to get their permission first.

Randy created clever ways to hide these essentials, probably from a few ideas he picked up at the Magic Kingdom. A wishing well conceals a water spigot, and some of the larger "rocks"—which are actually pieces of concrete that we shaped by hand—camouflage electrical outlets.

TOPS ON HER LIST

The brick patio was high on my wish list because it brought back great memories of our former home in Alexandria, Virginia. We had a beautiful patio there, and I'd longed for one just as nice ever since we moved.

Knowing this would probably be our last house, Randy went the extra mile and built an impressive 10- by 20-foot surface from salvaged chimney bricks. He laid the patio in a simple rectangular pattern for a reason—the chimney bricks were old, and no two were the same size. Some had as much as a 3/4-inch difference! Keeping the pattern simple was the answer to fitting this puzzle together.

Next we focused on the shady areas near the borders of our backyard. Summer gets blistering down here, so we built a wooden deck, grilling area and platform for our glider so we could make the most of this cooling shade.

Randy works on one area at a time until it's complete. After the grunt work is done, I fill in the flowering things. Randy even built me a potting bench below a large shade tree, so I can work in the coolest part of the yard.

It's Randy's thrifty nature that made our plants so prolific. As soon as we decided to move, he started digging, dividing and potting perennials that would transplant easily and grow fast at our new home.

Randy's a scavenger, too. When a nearby bank was renovated, Randy noticed a grounds crew removing the old plants. He asked what would happen to them, found out they were destined for the trash, and asked if he could have some. The workers said, "Sure—as long as you beat the garbage truck."

Randy scurried home, hooked up his trailer and returned to load as many plants as he could haul. We didn't even recognize some of them, but we planted them where we thought they'd work best, and most of the time we were right.

Randy also bought plants from a man who was changing the landscaping on his property. A newspaper ad invited the public to dig up the old plants for 35¢ each! As you can imagine, Randy was among the first to arrive.

We've accomplished a lot in just a few years. It's been a lot of work, but with most of the big projects complete, we have more time to sit back and enjoy the backyard magic. ❦

HERE'S THE
(plan)

1. Fig tree
2. Caladium
3. Majestic palm
4. Azalea
5. Ivy
6. Boxwood
7. Elm
8. Sago palm
9. Wishing well
10. Daylily
11. Indian hawthorn

12. Geranium
13. Asparagus fern
14. Border grass
15. Grill
16. Fern
17. Oak
18. Violet
19. Norfolk Island pine
20. Two-seat glider
21. Golden-rain tree
22. Crape myrtle

BUDGET SECRET:

$

Stay alert for plant bargains. When Randy spotted a grounds crew removing existing plants at a bank, he saved them from the trash bin—and put them in his own backyard.

mail-order
MAKEOVER

BY KATHY AND TED OREAN
OMAHA, NEBRASKA

INEXPENSIVE CATALOG PLANTS GAVE HER BACKYARD A FRESH NEW LOOK.

In the beginning, my plan was simple. We had just moved into our new home, and the landscape was fairly plain, with just a few hedges, some hostas and an old apple tree.

My main goals were to gain a little privacy for the patio and provide some shade in the backyard. But it didn't stop there. Before I knew it, I was reading gardening books, and my mind was racing as I pictured all the things that could be done with my blank slate. I wanted the kind of yard that begged you to take a stroll.

I began looking through plant catalogs, eager to find the perfect shrubs and flowers for my area. It was wonderful. I loved the convenience, variety and price of ordering plants by mail.

Then one day, I realized it had happened. There was no denying it and no turning back—gardening had drawn me in for good. And my mail-ordering days had just begun.

That was 10 years ago. Since then, my husband, Ted, and I have come a long way.

In those first few months, we were mostly concerned with improving the front yard.

Ted does concrete work, and he got busy right away laying a new driveway, front sidewalk and steps. While he was doing that, I was relocating numerous hostas and yews from the front yard to other areas. It was then that I noticed my passion for "digging in" and giving plants new homes.

MOVING OUT BACK

As we shifted our efforts to the backyard, Ted continued working on construction projects, and I kept on planting. Using concrete, he designed walkways and an octagon-shaped pad for a gazebo he built from a kit.

The results were amazing. Ted had turned our ordinary space into a parklike setting. It was up to me to add the finishing touches. He could barely get his projects complete before I was rushing in to soften the landscape with colorful plants like chrysanthemums, goatsbeard and burning bush.

I take pride in the fact that Ted and I have done all of the work on our own. He always seems to be crafting something impressive, and I have also taken on projects beyond planting. I installed all of the pavers in our yard myself, and I've created several garden structures, from a mosaic birdbath to several copper trellises and an arbor designed from PVC pipe.

BARGAINS THROUGH THE MAIL

If you look around my yard, you'll quickly notice my love for shrubs and ornamental grasses. They hold up year-round, and more importantly, provide shelter for wildlife.

I can't imagine an area without my backyard friends. It's such a treat to listen to all the dif-

Kathy installed pavers to create inviting, parklike paths.

3

HERE'S THE
(plan)

1. Arborvitae
2. Yew
3. Coreopsis
4. Ornamental grass
5. Coralbells
6. 'Blue Muffin' viburnum
7. Dwarf burning bush
8. Forsythia
9. Juniper
10. 'Green Velvet' boxwood
11. Spirea
12. 'Little Henry' sweetspire

13. 'Minuet' weigela
14. Butterfly bush
15. Chrysanthemum
16. Crabapple
17. Topiary spruce
18. 'Blue Mist' caryopteris
19. Hydrangea
20. Variegated dogwood
21. Goatsbeard
22. Privet hedge

BUDGET SECRET: $

Ordering plants from catalogs can save money, especially during end-of-season sales. It's also a good way to find plants your local nursery doesn't offer.

ferent birdsongs while the squirrels are chattering away.

My love for these creatures started with a single birdbath and quickly expanded from there. I couldn't keep the one I had filled, so I added more. Now I have seven baths as well as four birdfeeders, two squirrel feeders and several birdhouses (which are always filled with nestlings in spring).

Nearly all the plants and shrubs for my feathered friends have come from mail-order catalogs. I was skeptical of this method at first. But I decided to give it a try after I couldn't find a specific variety of privet hedge at my local greenhouse. I ordered the shrubs, and they came right to my door, healthy and strong.

I've been using mail order ever since. It saves me in cost, especially with those end-of-season specials, and everything I've ever received has thrived in my garden. Plus, it gives me

something to do in the winter.

I love pouring through the catalogs, searching for more plants and ideas. It's about this time—when I get a faraway look in my eyes—that Ted breaks into my daydream.

"You know, I'm not sure how much more we can add to the yard," he'll say with a knowing smile.

"There's always more room," I assure him.

SIGN SAYS IT ALL

It's funny how you discover new interests. I never would have imagined that gardening would be such a big part of my life, but I wouldn't have it any other way.

I love spending my free time outdoors. When anyone who knows me comes to visit, they always stop by my backyard first. In fact, the sign of my front porch reads, "If no answer, come to the garden."

I never get tired of the work involved. Anytime I try to sit down for a moment, the sights and sounds beckon me to become a part of them. Maybe someday I'll actually kick back and relax, but for now, I'm enjoying myself too much. ❦

The Oreans worked together to create a relaxing backyard getaway.

welcome to the NEIGHBORHOOD

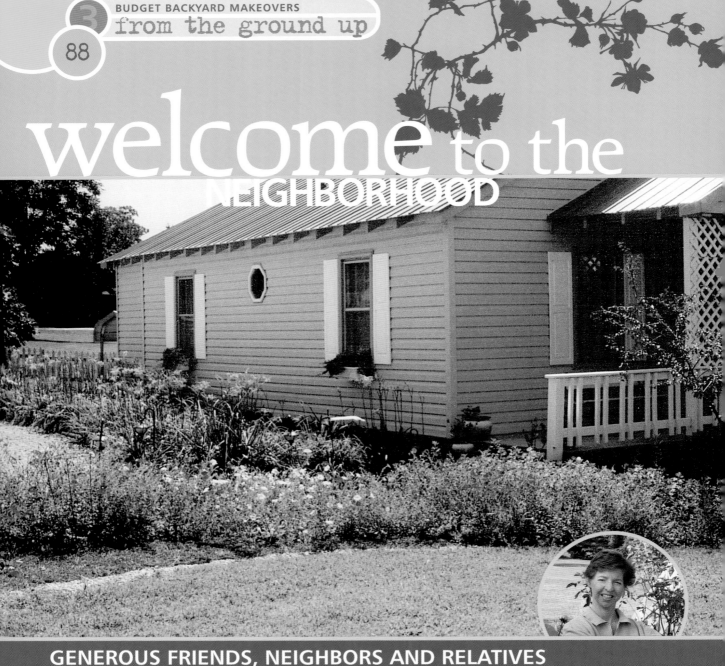

GENEROUS FRIENDS, NEIGHBORS AND RELATIVES HELPED HER GARDEN GROW.

BY BRENDA HILL
ROYSTON, GEORGIA

Unimpressive—that's probably the kindest thing you could've said about my yard when I bought my home in 1995.

My mother tried to be optimistic, saying I could add some trees here and flowers there.

Since the house also needed work, there was little money left for plants. Fortunately, Southerners believe in the old adage, "If you want your garden to grow, you have to give it away."

As I began work on my garden, one sister gave me daylilies and irises. Another mailed liriope and mondo grass from Texas. My parents contributed dogwoods, sedum, sweet William and more irises and daylilies.

JUST BEING NEIGHBORLY

As neighbors saw me working in the yard, they offered more garden goodies: hollyhocks, nandina, 'Autumn Joy' sedum, bush honeysuckle, petunias, roses, crape myrtle, daffodils, plum trees, flowering quince…the list goes on and on.

I often came home to find a bag of plants on the back porch and had to ask around for the contributor!

I did purchase a few key items—a couple of 'Bradford' pear trees and four crape myrtles. These reduce noise and provide screening from

Plus, it breaks down during the year and enriches my clay soil.

This garden has been a work in progress for 7 years. I extended many smaller flower beds and then connected them together.

ON A TIGHT BUDGET

To keep my gardening within a reasonable budget, I try to limit my expenses to one major project each year.

> "I often came home to find a bag of **plants** on the porch and had to ask around for the contributor."

the nearby road and business center. I also bought a corkscrew willow to mark the corner of my property.

With all this blooming bounty coming in, I had to make plans quickly and learn along the way.

My first step was to put in a gravel drive and edge it with landscape timbers to keep the gravel in place.

Next, I needed to find mulch that wouldn't wash away. After several unsuccessful attempts, a neighbor suggested pine straw. And, as luck would have it, she had some under her pines!

The pine straw looked great and stayed put.

One year, my nephew and his father helped me build a 180-foot picket fence. Another summer, my sister and I built trellises for my climbing roses. A prefab barn, courtesy of my nephew and his dad, was a recent big summer project.

Birthday gifts have become rakes, a shovel, hoe and lopping shears.

I made the stepping-stones, path borders and my patio from recycled bricks and pieces of granite. Leftover wrought-iron railing became low trellises for variegated vinca. Found rocks and driftwood became interesting accents.

DIVIDE AND CONQUER

Most of the plants I purchase are bulbs or rhizomes that multiply and can be divided later. And I usually buy just one or two plants a year.

My cannas near the back fence are a good example. I started with eight plants about 6 years ago. Now those flowers fill an area 50 feet long.

I also look for plants that have more than one in the container so I can separate them and get more for my money, and I look for end-of-the-season deals.

As long as you aren't too choosy about color, texture or size, you can create a wonderful cottage garden—complete with memories of family and friends.

Photograph and label the contributions each

BUDGET SECRET:

$

Be a smart shopper. "Most of the plants I purchase are bulbs or rhizomes that multiply and can be divided later," Brenda says. "I usually buy just one or two plants a year."

year, and you'll soon have albums full of floral keepsakes to get you through the cold, bare months of winter.

I use these to decide what needs to be moved the following season, or to determine what extra plants I have to swap in spring.

It also helps me remember whom to thank for their blooming contributions to my once-unattractive plot. ❦

BUDGET SECRETS:

When she buys new plants, Brenda looks for pots with more than one plant in the container so she can separate them and get more for her money.

Recycle wrought-iron railings into low trellises for vining plants. **$**

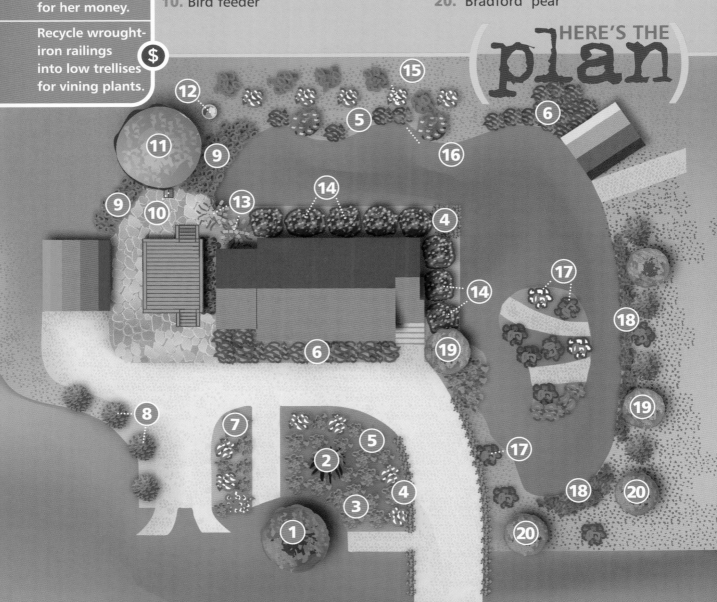

1. Dogwood
2. Ornamental grasses
3. Petunia
4. Liriope
5. Nandina
6. Daylily
7. Rose-of-Sharon
8. Crape myrtle
9. Canna
10. Bird feeder
11. Willow
12. Birdbath
13. Forsythia
14. Barberry
15. Sedum
16. Bush honeysuckle
17. Rose
18. Siberian iris
19. Plum
20. 'Bradford' pear

HERE'S THE (plan)

path
IN A
WHEELBARROW

THERE'S NO HEAVY LIFTING, NO FANCY TOOLS AND IT'S REALLY, REALLY CHEAP!

BY GREGG CARLSEN
STILLWATER, MINNESOTA

This garden path is as easy to build as it is to look at and walk on. All you need to build it is a bundle or two of cedar shakes, a roll of landscape fabric, a few bags of mulch and a couple of hours. That's it!

To create the path edging, we cut 18-inch-long cedar shakes in half, then pounded the 9-inch sections about halfway into the ground. Shakes are naturally rot-resistant and should last 5 to 10 years or more. And since they're tapered, they're easy to install.

Bear in mind, shakes will split and break if you try to pound them into soil that has lots of rocks, roots or heavy clay. This path works best in a garden setting with loose soil.

The landscape fabric helps prevent weeds from growing up into the path, and creates a barrier so the dirt below remains separate from the path materials above.

The path material itself can be wood chips, shredded bark, decorative stone—just about anything! ❧

! BUILDING TIP: If the shakes break as you drive them in, place a scrap 2x6 on top of each shake and pound on that. The 2x6 will help distribute the blow more evenly across the top of the shake.

HERE'S HOW TO DO IT IN THREE STEPS:

1 Pound the cedar shakes into the soil using a small mallet. Stagger every other shake, overlapping the previous shake by about 1/2 inch.

2 Trim or fold the fabric so it follows the contour of the cedar shake edging. On sloped ground, use U-shaped sod staples to hold the fabric.

3 Install a 2- to 3-inch layer of wood chips, shredded bark or stone over the landscape fabric.

BRIGHTideas

HAPPY TRAILS

Think your budget can't accommodate an appealing backyard path? Maybe it can! These one-of-a-kind designs run the gamut from casual, cottage-garden trails to formal, manicured walkways, but they all have one thing in common—a bargain-basement price tag.

please stay on the grass
Most home owners remove grass to make a walkway, but in this yard, the grass is the path. Planters, shrubs and mulch define the winding path that leads to a fountain in Brenda Sensenig's Ephrata, Pennsylvania backyard. Brenda fills the planters with fast, lush growers like dragon-wing begonias, and prunes the arborvitae between them into unique shapes.

heavy traffic Jan and Dave Kragen of Bainbridge Island, Washington built this path with recycled roadbed from a street-building project, breaking the asphalt into small chunks and filling the gaps with concrete. The paths hold up well in the mild coastal climate. In a decade, they've needed only a power-washing to flush out broken bits and a quick patch job with concrete mix. The Kragens have spent only $200 to $300 for 400 square feet of paths, and each load of asphalt they scavenge saves the city at least $70 in hauling and dumping fees. The coolest feature? On moonlit nights, the reflective traffic lines give off a soft glow.

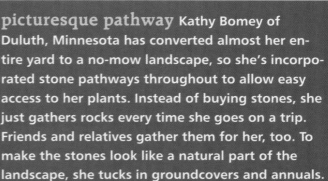

picturesque pathway Kathy Bomey of Duluth, Minnesota has converted almost her entire yard to a no-mow landscape, so she's incorporated stone pathways throughout to allow easy access to her plants. Instead of buying stones, she just gathers rocks every time she goes on a trip. Friends and relatives gather them for her, too. To make the stones look like a natural part of the landscape, she tucks in groundcovers and annuals.

keeping it simple
To make her large garden more manageable, Peggy Moen divided it into several small plots, then created a maze of walkways by simply laying down a mulch of old hay. "This keeps everything neat and tidy, and the hay nourishes the soil as it breaks down," says Peggy, of Foxboro, Wisconsin. "The plants along the edge of the border look just great." This method also keeps the garden layout flexible, so it's easy to rearrange plots and paths.

BRIGHTideas

BEAUTY ON A BUDGET

Sticking to a budget can be especially difficult when your yard is the landscaping equivalent of a blank slate. There's so much space to fill…and it all costs money, right? Not necessarily. These home owners share their tips for backyard beauty on a shoestring budget.

take a seat

This wooden chair came from a South Carolina schoolhouse where Ginny Dubose's mother once worked. Now it's a gracious plant stand for annual vinca in Ginny's Savannah, Georgia backyard.

cut-rate cascade Joe Bell of Markham, Ontario wanted a birdbath fountain, but balked at the cost of commercial ones, so he designed his own—for a fraction of the cost. He used oil pans with spouts for the "baths" and a plastic covered storage bin for the water reservoir. The plant and birdbath pedestals were free for the asking at a nearby conservation area. Strategically placed flowers conceal the network of bins, hoses and electrical connections.

on a roll Vintage farm implements are among Jack and Judy Boxx's favorite plant containers. Their front yard near Bellingham, Washington sports a milk cart filled with roses and geraniums. They're also fond of a rusty child's wagon that overflows with petunias, pansies and lobelia.

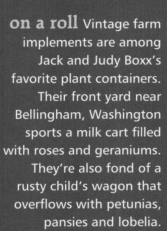

an early start When you have a large gardening space, you want to fill it fast. Jeff Nowak of Franklin, Wisconsin created this mini greenhouse for his bedding plants in just 15 minutes. He sandwiched the cover, a heavy-duty plastic drop cloth, between pieces of scrap 2x4s and attached the top section to his fence. "On nice days, I just rolled the cover up and hung it on the ladder hooks," Jeff says. Total cost: Less than $5.

FOOLPROOF PLANTS TO
JUMP-START YOUR GARDEN
annuals

CALIFORNIA POPPY
ESCHSCHOLZIA CALIFORNICA

Bloom time: All summer.

Light needs: Full sun.

Mature plant size: 8 to 12 inches high and wide.

Care tip: Allow California poppies to self-sow, and you'll have plenty in years to come.

MORNING GLORY
*IPOMOEA PURPUREA
AND CULTIVARS*

Bloom time: Summer.

Light needs: Full sun.

Mature plant size: 5 to 10 feet high and wide.

Care tip: Overwatering leads to rampant, lanky growth.

COSMOS
COSMOS BIPINNATUS

Bloom time: All summer.

Light needs: Full sun.

Mature plant size: 2 to 5 feet high, up to 2 feet wide.

Care tip: Overly rich ground leads to floppy growth, so plant in average soil.

IMPATIENS
*IMPATIENS 'WALLERIANA'
CULTIVARS*

Bloom time: Spring and summer.

Light needs: Full to partial shade.

Mature plant size: 6 inches to 2 feet high and 1 to 2 feet wide.

Care tip: Superb in shady or partially shaded area with moist soil.

NASTURTIUM
TROPAEOLUM MAJUS

Bloom time: All summer.

Light needs: Full sun.

Mature plant size: Up to 15 inches high and wide.

Care tip: Nasturtiums adore full sun. Climbing and trailing ones are easy to train.

WHEN YOU NEED TO FILL IN A BARREN AREA IN A HURRY, PLANTS WITH LOTS OF COLOR ARE JUST THE TICKET. YOU CAN'T MISS WITH THIS COMBINATION OF BOUNTIFUL ANNUALS AND PERENNIALS.

perennials

HOSTA
HOSTA SPECIES AND CULTIVARS

Bloom time: Varies with cultivar.

Light needs: Full to partial shade.

Hardiness: Zones 3 to 9.

Mature plant size: Varies with cultivar.

Care tip: Rich, moist soil is ideal...but be on the lookout for slugs and snails.

BUGLEWEED
AJUGA REPTANS

Bloom time: Late spring to early summer.

Light needs: Full sun to partial shade.

Hardiness: Zones 4 to 8.

Mature plant size: 4 to 8 inches high, 8 inches wide.

Care tip: Plant closely so it forms a dense, weed-suppressing mat.

LILY
LILIUM SPECIES AND HYBRIDS

Bloom time: Summer; varies with cultivar.

Hardiness: Zones 5 to 9.

Mature plant size: 2 to 7 feet high, 1 to 2 feet wide.

Care tip: Plant in fall or mid-spring for fast growth beginning in late spring.

WINDFLOWER
ANEMONE BLANDA

Bloom time: Spring.

Light needs: Full sun to partial shade.

Hardiness: Zones 4 to 8.

Mature plant size: 6 inches high and wide.

Care tip: Well-drained, slightly alkaline soil is best.

DAHLIA
DAHLIA HYBRIDS

Bloom time: Late summer and fall.

Light needs: Full sun.

Hardiness: Zones 7 to 10.

Mature plant size: 2 to 5 feet high, 1 to 2 feet wide.

Care tip: Plant in spring. Prevent rot by growing in soil that drains well.

making the grade

WITH STONES FROM AN OLD BARN FOUNDATION, THEY CREATED AN "OUTDOOR LIVING ROOM" FOR JUST $625.

LEVELING THE
playing field

BY MICHELLE AND RICH JURGENS
HOPKINTON, IOWA

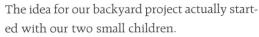

"A wheel rim from an old tractor made a **perfect enclosure** for the fire pit..."

BUDGET SECRET:

Michelle bought only one plant for her new backyard. "We simply divided and moved plants around from other parts of the yard," she says.

$

The idea for our backyard project actually started with our two small children.

Anna and Will loved going on camping trips, but my husband and I preferred to spend weekends at home, working around the yard. Buying a tent and building a backyard fire pit was the perfect compromise. We could spend our weekend nights under the stars and still putter in the yard during the day.

There were just two problems—a drastic slope to the yard, and a very limited budget. How could we turn our yard into the perfect campsite and outdoor living room, when we couldn't even set up a lawn chair without it tipping over?

I spent all winter thinking about it. Then it hit me. Our property in east-central Iowa had a stone foundation from an old barn. Why not use those rocks to build retaining walls to level the slope? We could create a patio with a fire pit and save big money by doing it ourselves.

DIGGING IN

By spring, Rich and I were digging out an area in the middle of the yard to make a base for the patio. At the low end of the slope, we built a rock retaining wall, making the patio

almost level with the top of the rise.

We brought in fill to raise the patio area, then added a gravel base for the stonework. As we worked, we leveled constantly to make sure we didn't have low spots. This was a project we wanted to get right the first time.

A wheel rim from an old tractor made a perfect enclosure for the fire pit. We placed it in the middle of the patio, and a blacksmith friend made a metal frame around it for added safety.

When the patio base was as level as we could get it, we started placing large rocks to make it look like a flagstone patio. They were big and heavy, and we needed a skid loader to move

them. It was back-breaking work. The rocks were all different sizes and shapes, so we had to do lots of digging and shaping to place each one. This job alone took an entire week!

To hold the rocks in place, we poured concrete into the gaps. I wanted to make the concrete less noticeable, so I pressed in tiny landscaping rocks as we filled each crack. That

The Jurgens family's **new backyard** is ideal for relaxing, entertaining, and even camping.

Rich and Michelle used extra stones to create this dry creek, which diverts water from the play area. A blacksmith friend made a frame for the fire pit on the patio (above).

HOUSE

1. Pergola
2. Spirea
3. Dwarf lilac
4. Herb garden
5. Black-eyed Susan
6. Drain
7. Fire pit
8. Potentilla
9. Yew
10. Hosta
11. Sedum
12. Daylily
13. 'Diablo' ninebark
14. Rock bench
15. Perennial bed
16. Dry creek bed

HERE'S THE (plan)

process took 10 hours. Boy, did my knees ache!

We included a small slotted drain to keep water from flowing down the hill and settling on the patio in winter. Terraced rock walls helped tame the slope, and a stepping-stone pathway from the top of the yard leads to the children's play area at the bottom.

Next, we divided and moved plants from other parts of the yard. The only shrub we bought was a 'Diablo' ninebark, which we put by the patio. I added an herb garden near the back door, sectioning it off with leftover rocks.

We had so many leftover rocks that we created a dry creek bed at the bottom of the yard to prevent flooding in the play area, and used the rest to edge planting areas. I can mow right up to the edges without lots of trimming.

We used barn wood to make chairs, and an old bed frame to make a garden bench——which sits on a patio we built from salvaged bricks. We landscaped around our shed with railroad ties from the dump.

Recycling saved us a bundle. The only items we bought were landscape rocks, gravel, cement mix, stepping-stones, some lawn furniture, lighting and that lone bush. The final tab: Just $625 for a complete backyard upgrade! ❧

$ BUDGET SECRET:

Recycle an old door as a design element—and put it to work. Michelle and Rich put one of these next to their shed and added hooks to the back for holding—and hiding—the garden hose and watering can.

TAKING IT TO the bank

HARD WORK TURNED A CRUMBLING HILLSIDE INTO A BLOOMING BACKYARD OASIS.

BY DANIEL AND WYOLENE SIMS
LAWRENCEVILLE, GEORGIA

Daniel built a retaining wall and raised beds to hold the slope's soil in place.

Caught between a rock and a hard place. That's how my wife, Wyolene, and I felt about our backyard when we moved into our new home northeast of Atlanta a few years ago.

The gently downward-sloping lot we'd chosen to build on was charming in the beginning. But during construction, our builders hit bedrock—or came awfully close! When they were finished, they left behind tons of stones, some clay and a hulking 8-foot-tall dirt wall.

When it rained, rivers of muddy water raged down the hill in a semicircle, plus a small pond and a rock waterfall. I never had to worry about running out of building materials. Everywhere I worked, I dug up more rocks.

I made a berm at the back of our lot to help raise the plants' roots above the rain-saturated soil. My efforts washed away twice, but the third time was the charm.

Once those hardscape features were in place, we hauled in topsoil to repair the bank and create a slope for flowers, trees and shrubs.

"I never had to worry about running out of building

BUDGET SECRET:

Lots of rocks at your place? Put 'em to work. Daniel used his to build a retaining wall, waterfall and pond.

$

past the house and washed away anything we tried to plant. Instead of creating the garden of our dreams, we were faced with a disaster that could ultimately damage our house.

Something had to be done. I drew upon the landscape design skills I'd learned in the U.S. Forest Service and created a master plan. My goals were simple but ambitious—I wanted to combat the erosion problem and turn our backyard mess into something we could enjoy.

SHORING UP THE YARD

The first step was to gather rocks for a retaining wall. We piled up all the stones on our property, then hunted down more in our neighborhood before I began to piece together a rustic barrier designed to keep the dirt in place.

Wyolene helped me select and place the stones. It was like putting together a puzzle. If one piece didn't fit, another one would.

Along the way, I added steps that wind

(in progress)

When the heavy lifting was complete, we started planting. We topped the berm with a pair of dogwoods, a 'Bradford' pear tree and two Yoshino cherries, and planted creeping phlox along the wall and the stone stairways.

I also built arbors over the steps for climbing 'New Dawn' roses. To dress up the ends of the wall and further anchor the soil, Wyolene and I created rose beds and planted more pear trees.

The new incline behind the rock wall needed the most attention. This was the trouble spot that sparked all this work, and I wanted to make sure the bank was going to stay in place. We covered it with annuals and perennials, from impatiens to elephant's ear.

All this hard work took just a little over a year. We've since added many more shrubs and trees. Today, we probably have more than 100 different varieties of flowers, bushes and trees.

The view from our screened porch is breathtaking for almost the entire year.

It was heartbreaking to watch new plantings wash away and then replace them, but I learned to respect the power of Mother Nature. And I'm glad we had no choice but to add topsoil. The shrubs, trees and flowers wouldn't have survived in the rocky clay without it. ❦

HERE'S THE
plan

1. Impatiens (summer) and pansy (fall and spring)
2. Japanese maple
3. Elephant's ear
4. Azalea
5. Hosta
6. Gardenia
7. Boxwood
8. Arbor with 'New Dawn' rose
9. Tea rose
10. 'Knockout' rose
11. Abelia
12. Pine
13. Dogwood
14. Creeping phlox
15. Ornamental pear
16. Yoshino cherry

materials. **Everywhere** I worked, I dug up rocks."

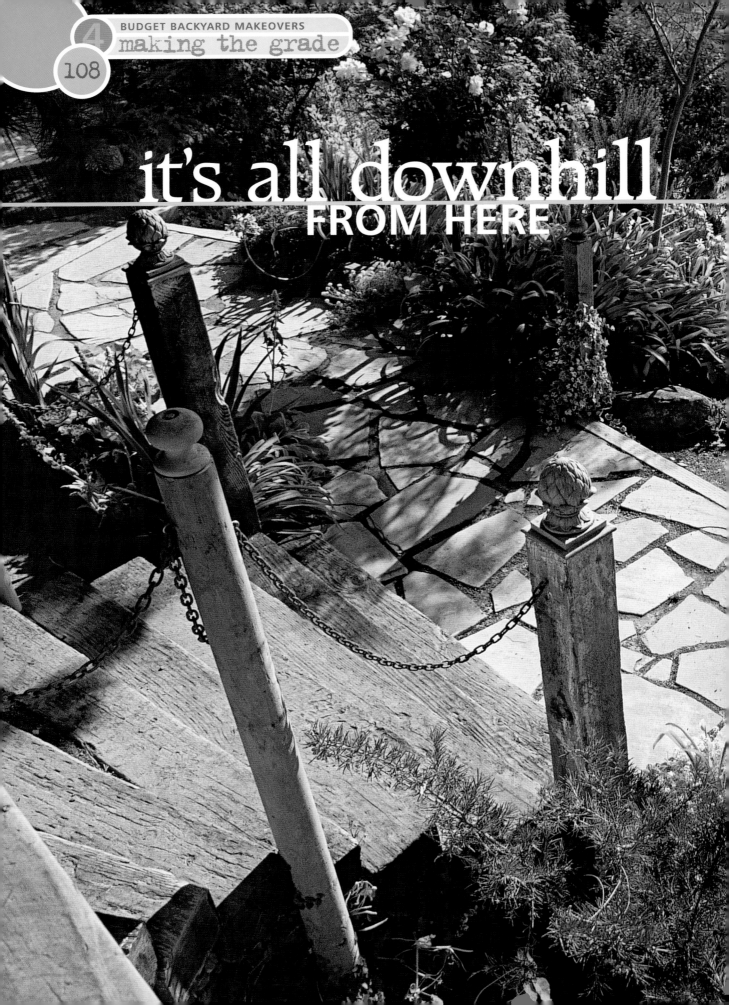

it's all downhill
FROM HERE

INSTEAD OF WAITING FOR THE "PERFECT" LAYOUT, HE TURNED A 45-DEGREE SLOPE INTO A SHOWPLACE.

BY BRIAN AND EILEEN BARRON
BENICIA, CALIFORNIA

When my wife and I bought our home in 1973, we never intended to stay forever. At retirement, we planned to buy a single-story cottage on a level piece of ground where I could indulge all my garden passions—arbors and winding brick walls...topiaries and trellises...roses and romance.

But Eileen and I still live in our house over-looking the Carquinez Straits north of San Francisco, where flat land is at a premium. It offers a beautiful view, but a less-than-ideal spot for gardening.

Our 1/3-acre suburban backyard was a grassy precipice. From the patio to the bottom of our lot, the elevation plummets three stories! One of my first tasks was building a rail to stop my small son from tumbling down the slope. He'd fallen a couple of times, and getting him back up was a little like a mountain rescue.

The wind is relentless up here, too. Eileen brought camellias from our previous yard, only to see their leaves ripped and shredded. The first lesson we learned was that if we wanted to grow any plants, they'd need protection.

I built a brick and wood partition with a tempered-glass windscreen to link the patio to the rest of the house and provide tender plants sanctuary without interrupting the view.

Finishing this project gave me untold confidence. After that, it was all downhill—literally.

TEETERING ON THE BRINK

Although my plan was to start my "final garden" somewhere less extreme, the desire to plant was overwhelming, and I couldn't wait to get started.

Blinded by sweat, teetering on the 45-degree

grade with a safety line knotted around my waist, I hacked planting cavities out of the adobe and shale soil with a pickax. I often wondered why we didn't just move. Nebraska had a lovely ring to it…

Clinging to the slope like a mountaineer, I planted trees and shrubs in pockets the size of party hats. It was humbling when I later had to cut most of them down. They were in the wrong place, blocking the view, and didn't fit into the garden plan beginning to form in my mind. Even

HERE'S THE
plan

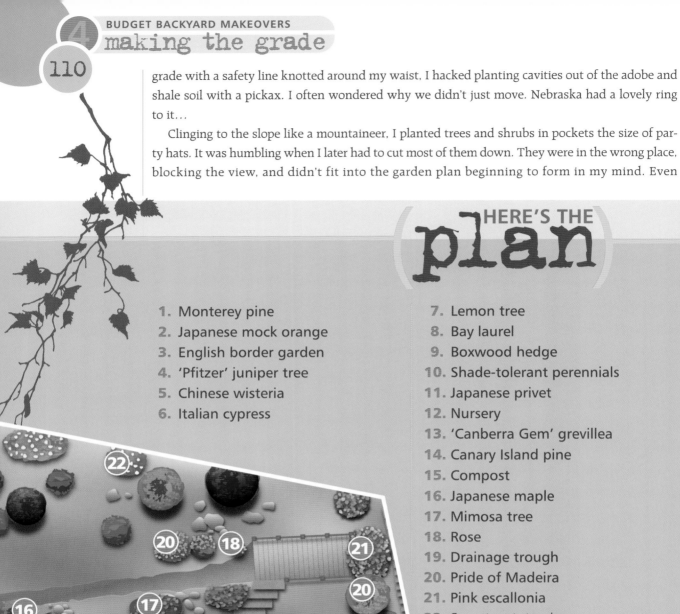

1. Monterey pine
2. Japanese mock orange
3. English border garden
4. 'Pfitzer' juniper tree
5. Chinese wisteria
6. Italian cypress
7. Lemon tree
8. Bay laurel
9. Boxwood hedge
10. Shade-tolerant perennials
11. Japanese privet
12. Nursery
13. 'Canberra Gem' grevillea
14. Canary Island pine
15. Compost
16. Japanese maple
17. Mimosa tree
18. Rose
19. Drainage trough
20. Pride of Madeira
21. Pink escallonia
22. Sweet potato vine

$ BUDGET SECRET:

Instead of digging planting holes, Brian now uses half wine barrels with drainage holes drilled in the bottom. "I sink them deeply into the slope, fill them with a good soil mix, and I'm ready to plant," he says. This saves the expense of amending poor soil, helps stabilize the grade and minimizes runoff.

An inviting arch opens onto a terrace in the Barrons' backyard. Below right: Brian needed a pickax to hack out these planting cavities (top); containers brighten the patio.

though it was a few years before my retirement I felt I could at least begin developing part of the hill.

I worked from the top down, slowly adding planting beds, steps and pathways so people could work their way down the slope to enjoy the gardens. I did all the carpentry, bricklaying and cement pouring myself.

I did most of the hauling, too. You can't use a wheelbarrow on a slope like this, and there's no way to drive around back and throw stuff over the fence. Everything must be carried up and down—soil fill, bricks, paving stones, weeds, trimmings.

Building terraces and retaining walls became second nature. For years, I used railroad ties, but now I like the new treated landscaping lumber. It's readily available and much easier to lug downhill.

A PROPER ENGLISH GARDEN

Eileen and I were raised in England, so the garden has a classical and romantic look. I included urns, pedestals, statuary, arches and manicured hedges, some in curving shapes that undulate down the hill. There's also an English border planted with old favorites like coreopsis, Shasta daisies, gladiolas and nasturtiums.

Since hardly anything else grows for long here without supplemental water, I installed my own irrigation layout using PVC pipes.

I retired in 1992, and finally accepted that I was never moving to that cottage on a flat piece of land. Rather than throw in the trowel, I rolled up my sleeves and decided to tackle the bottom part of the yard.

I started by building a rose arch, then concentrated on bringing the lower section of the garden into harmony with the upper part by creating terraces and adding new plantings. Then...a real setback.

El Niño rains caused a mudslide in our neighborhood. The rose arch slid into the neighbor's yard, along with the rest of my hard work. We lost 80 percent of our new landscaping, and 4 or 5 years of work.

No one was hurt, and our upper gardens were untouched, but it took a while to find the will to start landscaping on the lower 40 again. This time, we installed a trough running the width of our property for proper drainage.

Gardening here has been an adventure, and nature sometimes takes back as much as it gives. But when the evening light is at its golden best, I can turn to Eileen and say, "This is my garden. I did it, and I am pleased."

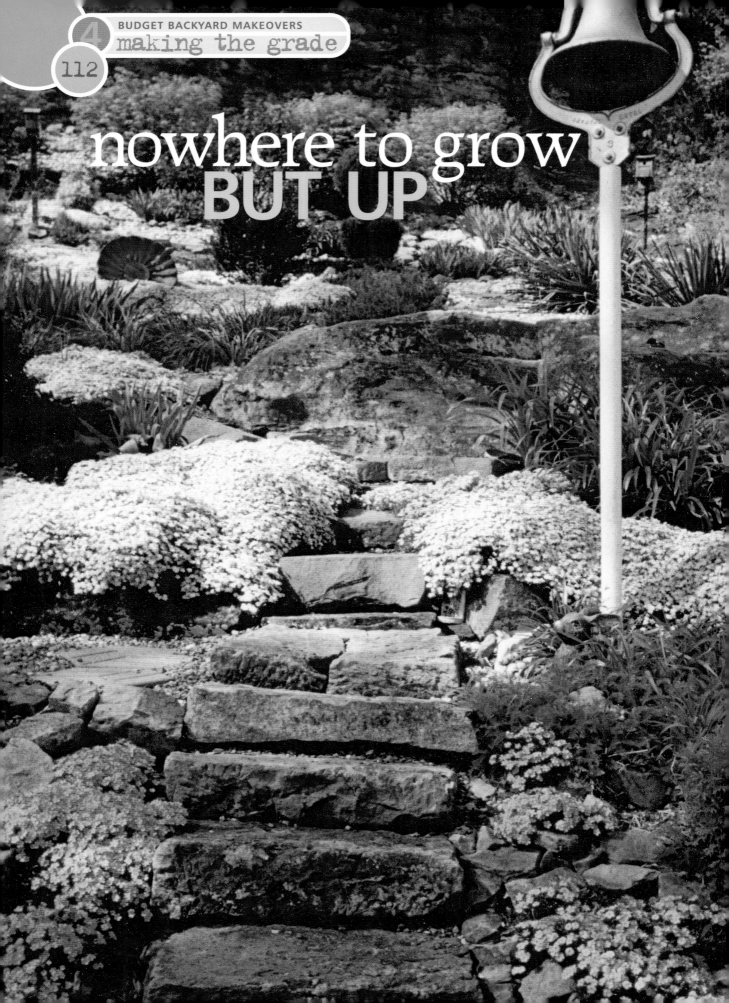

nowhere to grow
BUT UP

WITH A ROCKY SLOPE IN THE BACKYARD, PLANTING A LIVELY GARDEN WAS AN UPHILL BATTLE.

When we moved into our house in this Ohio River community in 1981, our "backyard" looked terrible. About 20 feet from our kitchen window stood a steep, rocky hill that climbed 77 feet to a cliff.

Jim wanted to clear the hill so we'd at least be able to mow it. But even after we removed the brush and briars, it was still filled with rocks—impossible to mow.

When our sons, Corey and Jacob, came along, they spent hours on the hill with their friends, digging out rocks to build forts. Jim and I started joking about turning the whole thing into a huge rock garden.

CLIMBING TOGETHER

Soon, I decided that was not such a crazy idea. I borrowed a few of the kids' rocks and outlined a small garden at the bottom of the hill. We liked it so much that Jim suggested we start making more of them in different shapes and slowly work our way up the slope.

Jim did most of the hard work. He moved the rocks around and gave the garden its outline, then we planted it together. With two small children and a tight budget, our only "couple time" was in the backyard with a bunch of rocks!

Our main goal was to cover the hillside with plants as quickly as possible. We put sheets of dark plastic everywhere to kill the weeds. Then we cleared away the plastic and started putting in plants, often one at a time. I never dreamed we'd actually make it to the top of the hill.

Friends, neighbors and relatives donated almost everything we planted. With such a large space to fill, we placed the plants far apart, hoping they'd eventually spread to fill in the gaps.

At first, many of the plants we chose would not

BY CHARLOTTE AND JIM CARRICO
HAWESVILLE, KENTUCKY

BUDGET SECRET: $

"After the spring bulbs begin to die back, I scatter zinnia and four-o'clock seeds to add color in the empty spaces," Charlotte says.

Patches of creeping phlox brighten the Carricos' hillside in spring. The angel that watches over their yard was an anniversary gift.

grow in the hard, rocky soil. And those that did grow often turned into tasty meals for the abundant wildlife that scampered through. But we didn't worry about that too much. It was hard enough just to find a few things that would survive, without wondering whether the hungry critters would eat them!

So we changed our focus and started searching for tough, hardy plants that were supposed to thrive "anywhere." We selected mostly groundcovers and had good luck with ivy, lily-of-the valley, bishop's weed, ajuga and creeping juniper. But beware—all these plants are fierce growers that don't care what's in their path.

And we planted a lot of creeping phlox. When it blooms in spring, it billows beautifully all over the hillside.

Once the groundcovers were in place, we started adding tulips, daffodils, perennials and shrubs. Now our backyard is filled with a wide array of plants, including iris, yucca, peony, azalea, rhododendron, baby's breath, foxglove, Jacob's ladder, coreopsis, forsythia, sweet William, euonymus and weigela, as well as dwarf holly. Things were starting to shape up!

BUDGET SECRET:

Look for plant bargains at yard sales. That's where Charlotte found her first hosta— for 75¢.

$

YARD SALE BARGAIN

Since there's a lot of shade, we loaded the hillside with hostas, too. I bought my first one at a yard sale for 75¢ and was surprised how easy it was to divide. We were so happy with them that we bought more.

One of my favorites, a huge yellow-leafed hosta, is planted among several burning bushes at the top of the hill. We also have some enormous yellow lilies up there that are visible from a mile away.

SCATTERING SEEDS

After the spring bulbs begin to die back, I scatter zinnia and four-o'clock seeds to add color in the empty spaces. To encourage our perennials to keep spreading, I deadhead the flowers and leave the dried blooms on the ground to reseed. (This works best with species plants; cultivars won't "come true" from seed, or may not grow at all.)

We've had many visitors stop by our yard in the last few years, especially after a TV station in Lexington aired a program about it. One couple got married at the church across the street and had some wedding photos taken here.

We're still not finished, though.

Groundcovers and tough plants turned a bare hillside into a showstopper. Now it's family tradition to take prom pictures there (left).

(before)

$ BUDGET SECRETS: To encourage perennials to keep spreading, Charlotte deadheads the flowers and leaves the dried blooms on the ground to reseed. This works best with species plants, which will "come true" from seed.

For spring color on a hillside, plant easy-care creeping phlox. It will spread each year, creating a dense mat of pretty blooms.

HERE'S THE
plan

1. Elm
2. Bishop's weed
3. Lily-of-the-valley
4. Peony
5. Creeping phlox
6. 'Blue Rug' juniper
7. Bell
8. Iris
9. Birdhouse
10. Barberry
11. Birdbath
12. Evergreen topiary
13. Azalea
14. Foxglove
15. Hosta
16. Lily
17. Euonymus

"One couple had some **wedding photos** taken here."

The garden will always be a work in progress.

Someday, we'd like to have stone steps all the way up the hillside. It may never happen—but then again, we never thought we'd get this far, and just look at how beautiful our backyard slope is now!

Our garden has become a special place filled with so many memories…of Jim and me working together…of our kids and their friends having fun gathering rocks…of all the kind people who've provided the plants we enjoy year after year.

Over time, this hillside has become part of our lives. 🌿

growing
WITH THE FLOW
SHE CREATED THIS CREEKSIDE RETREAT FOR UNDER $700.

Each time my husband, Rondy, cut the grass in our yard, he complained about the small flower beds I'd scattered across it. "It's like mowing an obstacle course," he'd grumble.

I knew something had to be done, but what? The rest of our Appalachian Mountain property sloped down to the creek, and that slope was covered in broom sage, an unsightly grass. Neither of us had ever considered gardening there before.

The more I thought about it, however, the more sense it made...and the more determined I became to cultivate the steep creek bank.

The only real limitation I faced was money. But the lack of it

BY TERESA PERDUE
ASHFORD, WEST VIRGINIA

served more as a motivator than a stumbling block. I knew I could make the most of my shoestring budget.

My mind made up, I asked my husband for the tools needed to clear the brush and prepare the creek bank for planting. He was on his way out for the day, and my request stopped him in his tracks. He stared at me, then shook his head and said, "Good luck," before bringing me a few shovels and a posthole digger.

Arms filled with the tools, I headed out to the creek bank, confident that I could tame it quickly. Little did I know how hard this was going to be!

TOUGH BREAKS

The brawny roots of broom sage grew so deeply that I couldn't pry them out or cut through them easily. After a full day of sweating and toiling on that bank, I'd conquered only a very small section. I'd also managed to break the handles on all of the tools Rondy had given me. This was already getting expensive!

When he came home, Rondy surveyed my work and told me I was crazy to think I could turn the creek bank into a garden. I think he was secretly surprised that I hadn't given up yet.

He also recognized that I could use a hand. By the end of summer, we'd cleared enough space for a flower bed and a little white swing

(in progress)

I'd picked up at a yard sale for $5.

When the seed catalogs arrived at our house that winter, I pored through them, reading everything I could about flowers and foliage. At that point, I didn't know a perennial from an annual...but I was willing to learn!

Slowly, I selected what I thought would be suitable specimens for the bank, ranging from purple coneflowers and irises to Adam's needles, Shasta daisies, coreopsis and dianthus. I also spotted a special deal on weeping willow trees—buy one at $1.99 and get a second tree for 1¢—so I ordered a pair of those, too.

By spring, my precious seeds had arrived. I was so thrilled that I planted everything im-

BUDGET SECRET: Look for clearance sales in late spring and early fall. "You'll rarely pay more than a few dollars for anything, including rosebushes, shrubs and trees," Teresa says. "I've found 1-gallon potted plants at the end of summer for as little as 50¢."

mediately, including the pair of willow seedlings, which looked like sticks with straggly roots rather than the lush trees pictured in the catalog.

The plants were all so cute, but they hardly made a dent in the flower bed we'd created. Luckily, a new home improvement store with a garden center had just opened up nearby, and I found some pretty amazing deals that fit my budget just fine!

BRIDGING THE GAP

Although the flower bed soon took on a lush appearance at a very low cost, it would still be an uphill battle to transform the rest of the bank. There was plenty of stubborn broom sage yet to remove—and that's when I caught a big break I never could've predicted.

The West Virginia highway department informed us that they'd be replacing the old bridge that spanned the creek with a new two-lane concrete version. On the surface, it seemed like a horrible inconvenience, but it turned out to be a lifesaver.

BANKING ON IT

By the time the bridge was finished, the workmen had managed to also cover up some 50 feet of my bank—broom sage and all—with dirt. All I had to do was select more garden plants and start digging!

Over time, I've added outdoor furniture made by friends and child-size lawn furniture I found on sale at a local department store so our grandson Corey and his pals can enjoy playing in and around the creek. I also added a path made of concrete pavers that meanders down the hill and along the water.

We certainly saved money by doing the work ourselves. But I think I'm most pleased with the many bargains found along the way. Scouring local stores and garage sales for the best deals really paid off. The total bill for my backyard project was less than $700!

Even better are the rich rewards I receive each time family and friends gather by my creekside retreat and revel in the great outdoors. That's priceless! ❧

BUDGET SECRETS:

Dicker, and buy in bulk. When Teresa found 50 butterfly bushes marked down to $3 each, she talked the store manager into selling her the lot for $1 apiece.

Don't pay for packaging. "I look for bags of mulch that have split open," Teresa says. "Stores usually reduce the price because they appear damaged, but nothing's wrong with what's inside."

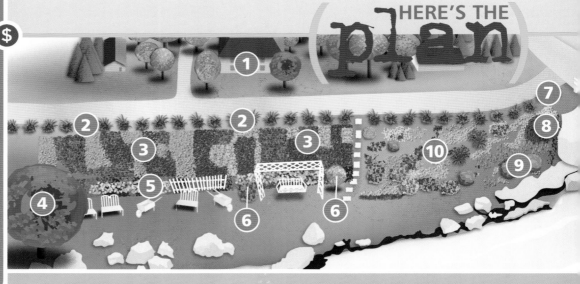

HERE'S THE plan

1. Perdue house
2. Butterfly bush
3. Creeping phlox
4. Weeping willow
5. 'Stella d'Oro' daylily
6. Honeysuckle vine
7. Rosebush
8. Spirea
9. Ajuga
10. Perennial garden

going for BROKE

HER NEW BACKYARD WAS A STEEP, OVERGROWN MESS—AND SHE LOVED THE CHALLENGE.

BY KELLY WALSH
SHELTON, CONNECTICUT

There's some good in poison ivy, stinging nettles and wild grapevines. They're the only things that kept my steep lawn from sliding into the Housatonic River!

I bought my small home in western Connecticut from someone who'd owned it for decades. The yard leading to the river was eroding, so I knew I had to do something before it was history.

> "Plant donations from **friends** and neighbors flooded in once they heard about our project."

The growth was so thick that it blanketed long-forgotten items like fence posts, a cable wheel, a metal drum, even a 25-foot section of rain gutter missing from the house. It was an overgrown, neglected mess…and I loved the challenge.

Buying the house left me nothing to spend but imagination and sweat. So I went for broke.

A road crew was widening the highway I took to work each day, so I routinely filled my trunk with rocks blasted from the roadside cliff.

After our wedding, my husband, Richard, caught rock fever, too. Before long, our side yard was a mountain of handpicked boulders for making stone walls.

After clearing the slope, I started terracing it for plants. I dug a trench for a retaining wall foundation, put the largest rocks I could handle in it, then staggered the next layers.

To fill in the back of the wall, I poured in small stones and packed in sandy soil. One wall after another, the bank began to take shape.

At a flower show, I ran into a seed company representative and told him about our project. Impressed with our enthusiasm, he gave us a shoebox full of seeds for $20. We started them indoors in anything that would hold soil. Then friends and neighbors donated plants—bishop's weed, hostas, 'Moonbeam' coreopsis, red-hot pokers, lilac shoots and more.

With a little help, we transformed this eroding slope into a beautiful backyard for less than $80—and that includes the $15 co-pay for a visit to the doctor to treat my poison ivy! 🌿

BUDGET SECRETS:

Ask for freebies at construction sites. "Bricks came from a demolition site, cobblestone from a nearby street project and slate from a church where the roof was being rebuilt," Kelly says.

Kelly makes her own mulch from newspaper, leaves and household vegetable scraps, then covers it with a thick layer of hay.

When Kelly bought her house, this slope was so overgrown it hid decades of debris, including a 55-gallon drum and a 25-foot section of rain gutter!

BRIGHTideas

ONE STEP AT A TIME

Containers, terraces, retaining walls and groundcovers can turn a bare hill into a striking display. If your yard doesn't have steps or pathways, make some with free or low-cost building materials. Then add easy-care plants that spread freely and require minimal maintenance (turn to pages 122-123 for suggestions), and wait for the compliments.

layers of color Do-it-yourselfers Brian Scheuch and his wife, Corinne Hajek, tamed their cliffside yard in LaConner, Washington by building up areas to create terraced flower gardens. In this part of their yard, they used a grape arbor, groundcovers and annuals to create lush layers of foliage and color.

flowers wall-to-wall Terracing solved Wess and Gertrude Hedrick's landscaping dilemma in Willow Grove, Pennsylvania. With help from son Chip, they built walls with fieldstones gathered at Gertrude's parents' farm. The stones were free, so the only cost was their time—and some sore muscles. "It was a long, arduous task, but the walls have stood for more than 25 years," Gertrude says. "They were well worth our effort."

working their way up To keep soil from washing down their Traverse City, Michigan slope, Dee and Stan Swanson placed landscape ties at the base and planted low-growing groundcovers to hold the soil in place and keep weeds at bay. They used the leftover ties to make twin paths up the hill, and then added trees, shrubs and flowers.

"Most of the flowers were cuttings from friends," says Dee. "The trees and shrubs were purchased at a discount at the end of the season."

front and center Flowerpots filled with colorful annuals brighten the steep stairway leading to Bonnie Moskowitz's front door in Bayside, New York. "I wanted the front yard to look as nice as the backyard, but the stairs looked really bare," Bonnie explained. "I added a few containers of flowers and they really warmed things up, so I kept adding more and more. They sure are pretty!"

PLANTS FOR TAMING THE
SLIPPERY SLOPE

DAYLILY
HEMEROCALLIS SPECIES AND CULTIVARS

Bloom time: All summer.

Light needs: Full to partial sun.

Hardiness: Zones 3 to 9.

Mature plant size: 2 to 4 feet high and wide.

Care tip: Give pastel colors some shade to help preserve their softer hues.

COTONEASTER
COTONEASTER HORIZONTALIS

Bloom time: Late spring to early summer.

Light needs: Full sun to partial shade.

Hardiness: Zones 4 or 5 to 7.

Mature plant size: 2 to 3 feet high and up to 7 feet wide.

Care tip: Performs best in loose, fertile soil. Attractive in full sun or light shade.

WILD ROSE
ROSA WICHURIANA

Bloom time: Early to midsummer.

Light needs: Full to partial sun.

Hardiness: Zones 5 to 8.

Mature plant size: 4 to 6 feet high and wide, or wider (trailing canes).

Care tip: Easy and trouble-free, but rampant once established.

ENGLISH IVY
HEDERA HELIX

Light needs: Full sun to heavy shade.

Hardiness: Zones 4 to 9.

Mature plant size: 6 to 8 inches high and widely spreading.

Care tip: Requires consistent pruning to keep in bounds. Struggles in hot, windy, exposed locations.

PACHYSANDRA
PACHYSANDRA TERMINALIS

Bloom time: Spring.

Light needs: Full to partial shade.

Hardiness: Zones 4 to 8.

Mature plant size: 6 to 10 inches high and 10 to 18 inches wide.

Care tip: Prefers full to partial shade (leaves turn yellow in full sun).

SLOPES ARE TRICKY TO MOW, WEED AND WATER. WHY NOT BYPASS GRASS AND PLANT SOMETHING MORE SELF-SUFFICIENT? THESE CHOICES SPREAD STEADILY—AND HOLD SOIL IN PLACE, TOO.

ROSEMARY
ROSMARINUS OFFICINALIS

Bloom time: Fall to spring.

Light needs: Full sun.

Hardiness: Zones 6 to 8 or 9.

Mature plant size: 2 to 4 feet high and wide.

Care tip: Prefers full sun. Don't overwater; rosemary will rot in damp soil.

PERIWINKLE/ TRAILING MYRTLE
VINCA MINOR

Bloom time: Spring to summer.

Light needs: Full sun to partial shade.

Hardiness: Zones 3 to 8 or 9.

Mature plant size: 4 to 8 inches high and broadly spreading.

Care tip: Cut back ends periodically to promote denser growth.

JAPANESE BARBERRY
BERBERIS THUNBERGII

Bloom time: Spring.

Light needs: Full sun.

Hardiness: Zones 4 to 8.

Mature plant size: 3 to 6 feet high and wide.

Care tip: Full sun is best. Dislikes damp ground.

HALL'S HONEYSUCKLE
LONICERA JAPONICA 'HALLIANA'

Bloom time: Early summer.

Light needs: Full to partial sun.

Hardiness: Zones 5 to 9.

Mature plant size: Between 15 and 30 feet high and wide (vine or groundcover).

Care tip: Don't fertilize; it grows rampantly. Plant where you can enjoy its scent.

ICE PLANT
DORSANTHEMUM SPECIES AND CULTIVARS

Bloom time: Late spring to summer.

Light needs: Full sun.

Hardiness: Zones 8 or 9 to 11.

Mature plant size: Up to 6 inches high and broadly spreading.

Care tip: Be aware that the flowers attract lots of bees.

mini shed
KEEPS HAND TOOLS HANDY

STORE YOUR GARDEN TOOLS WHERE YOU NEED THEM MOST—IN THE GARDEN.

RECOMMENDED TOOLS:

- ☐ Table saw
- ☐ Power drill
- ☐ Combination square

WHAT YOU NEED:

- ☐ 9 feet of 1-inch x 10-inch rough cedar
- ☐ 2 feet of 1-inch x 12-inch cedar
- ☐ 1-5/8-inch galvanized deck screws
- ☐ 2-inch and 1-1/2-inch galvanized finishing nails
- ☐ 7/8-inch wire brads
- ☐ Waterproof glue
- ☐ Four brass cup hooks
- ☐ Two small brass-plated hinges
- ☐ One decorative cabinet knob
- ☐ One clothespin
- ☐ One small wood screw
- ☐ One hook-and-eye assembly

Running back and forth to the garage for forgotten tools is nuisance enough in a flat yard. When your yard sits on a slope, those extra trips can turn into an unwelcome workout.

Cliff Muehlenberg of Pewaukee, Wisconsin created this miniature toolshed to save steps and keep his tools right where he needs them—in the garden.

The project can be completed in a few hours and takes only minutes to mount. It sits nicely atop a fence post, or can be attached to the back of a shed.

Cliff recommends building this shed from rough cedar. It costs a little more, but resists decay and never needs painting, so it's worth the extra expense.

This design accommodates most standard garden tools, but before you start building, check the lengths of your hand tools. If they're too long to fit in the shed (the interior dimensions are 22-5/8 inches from floor to peak), you can easily modify the design.

For your own safety, hang up your tools or secure them to the inside walls so they don't accidentally fall out when the door is opened. 🌿

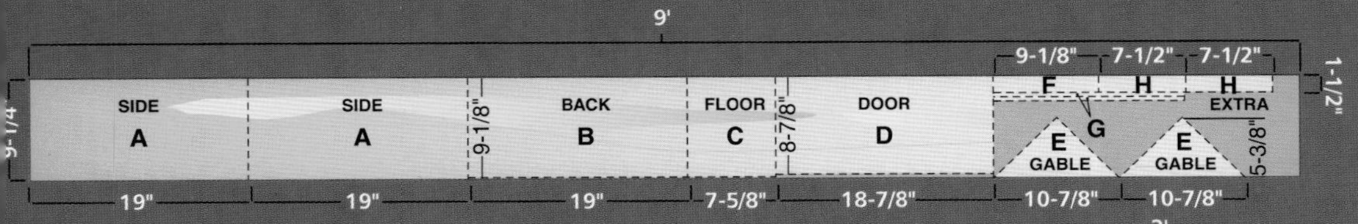

Board layout (top):

9'

SIDE A	SIDE A	BACK B	FLOOR C	DOOR D	F	H		

9-1/8" 7-1/2" 7-1/2"

9-1/4" 9-1/8" 8-7/8"

F   H   1-1/2"

E G E   EXTRA
GABLE   GABLE   5-3/8"

19"   19"   19"   7-5/8"   18-7/8"   10-7/8"   10-7/8"

9-1/8"

2'

LARGER ROOF I	SMALLER ROOF J	EXTRA

11-1/4"

11-1/4"   10-1/2"

time for your tools...

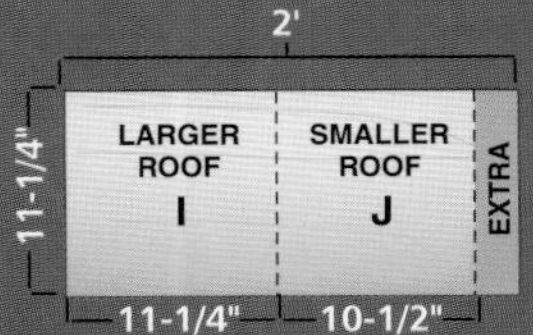

1. Cut the mini shed pieces by following the board layouts shown above and at right.

2. Center the gable support (piece F) on the smooth side of one gable. (This piece will be the front gable.) Then attach it with waterproof glue and 1-½-inch finishing nails so it extends ¾ inch below the bottom of the gable.

3. Assemble the back, sides and floor with glue and 2-inch finishing nails. Recess the floor ⅞ inch. Drill pilot holes first.

4. Attach the back gable to the back wall using glue and 1-½-inch finishing nails. Drill pilot holes near the ends of the piece before nailing to keep it from splitting.

5. Fasten the front gable with glue and 1-½-inch finishing nails. Attach it from the top of the gable to the sides of the shed. Then nail the sides to the gable support as shown in the plan.

6. Mount and glue the weather strips to the sides of the shed with ⅞-inch wire brads. Set them back ⅞ inch from the front edge of each side piece so they line up with the front edge of the floor. The door closes against the strips, which will keep rain from blowing in.

7. Screw four brass cup hooks into the inside walls to hold your tools.

8. Line up the roof pieces so that the larger piece overlaps the smaller. Predrill holes and attach them to the gables with glue and 1-½-inch finishing nails. (You may find it helpful to allow the glue to dry before nailing.)

9. Attach two braces to the inside of the door (positioning them as shown in the plan) with waterproof glue and 1-⅝-inch deck screws. Stagger the screws as shown. The braces keep the door from warping.

10. Fasten a clothespin with a small wood screw to the inside of the door (drill a pilot hole first) to hold a pair of garden gloves. Attach a decorative cabinet knob to the outside of the door. Then mount the door to the shed with two small brass-plated hinges.

11. Attach a hook-and-eye latch to the door to hold it closed.

12. Mount the shed on a post or a pole used for mounting a bird feeder. You also can hang it on a fence or on the outside wall of a garden shed or garage. Just add a 2 x 4 spacer to the back of the mini shed. Now gather up those tools and hang 'em up. Next time you're in the garden and need a trowel or hand pruner, it'll be a couple of steps away.

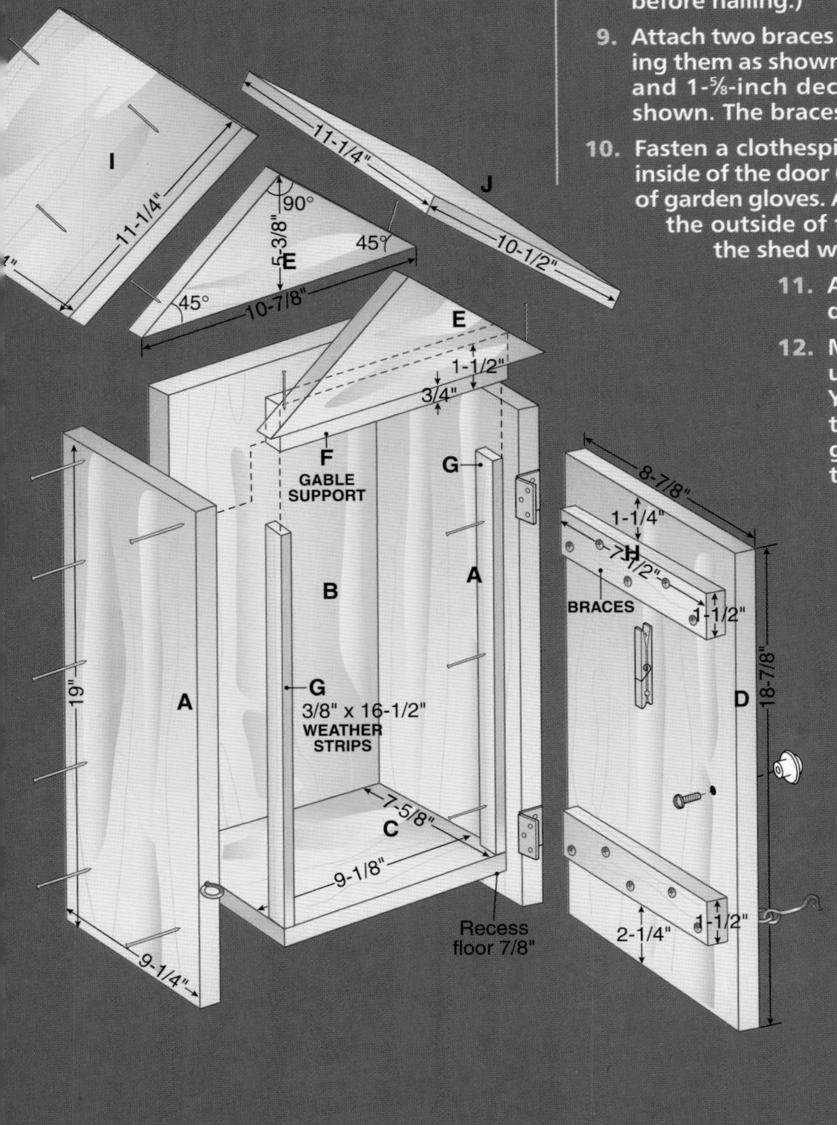

Assembly diagram labels:

I   11-1/4"   J   10-1/2"

11-1/4"   90°   5-3/8"   45°

45°   10-7/8"   E   E

1-1/2"   3/4"

F GABLE SUPPORT   G

B   A

G   3/8" x 16-1/2" WEATHER STRIPS

19"

A

7-5/8"

C

9-1/8"

9-1/4"

Recess floor 7/8"

8-7/8"

1-1/4"

H   7/8"

BRACES

1-1/2"

D

1-1/2"

2-1/4"   1-1/2"

18-7/8"

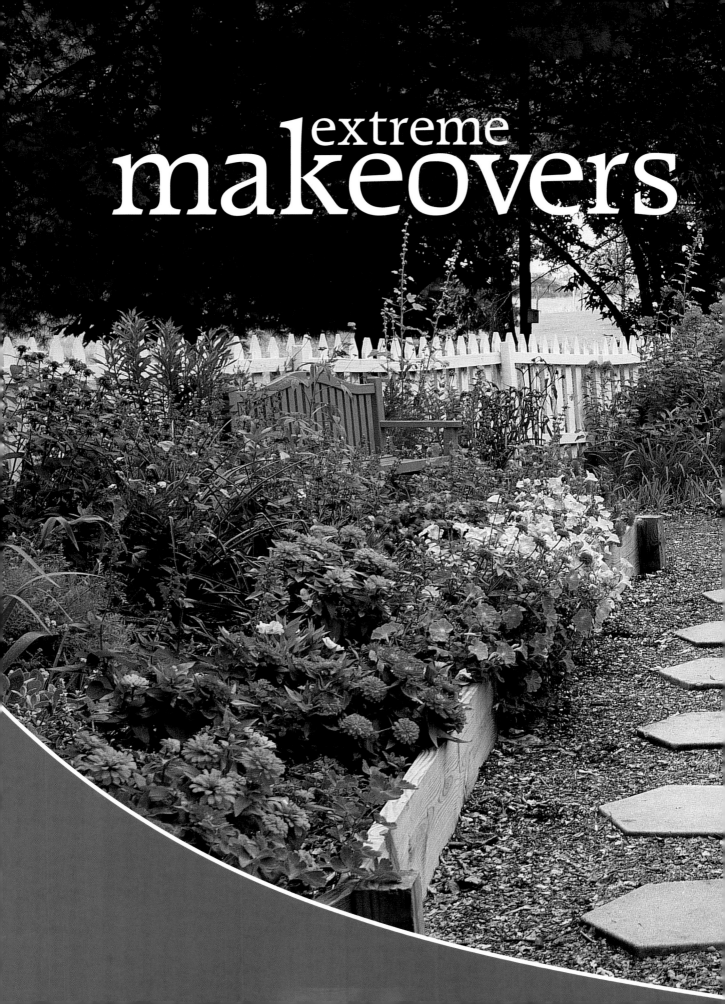

extreme
makeovers

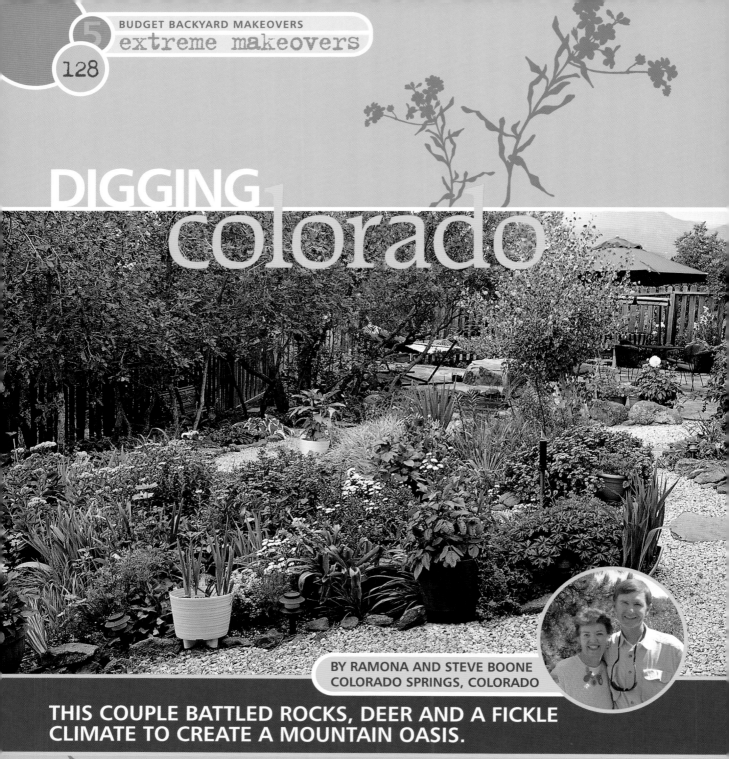

DIGGING colorado

BY RAMONA AND STEVE BOONE
COLORADO SPRINGS, COLORADO

THIS COUPLE BATTLED ROCKS, DEER AND A FICKLE CLIMATE TO CREATE A MOUNTAIN OASIS.

Living in Colorado has its advantages. My husband, Steve, and I enjoy breathtaking views of 14,000-foot mountains and fields of wildflowers. But as someone who grew up in Illinois, I couldn't stop dreaming of a lush, colorful garden filled with sweetly scented flowers.

Unfortunately, the deer that live near our home seemed to share the same dream. They regularly came down from the mountains to forage. Apparently, our 1-acre property was a great place to snack and nap!

As a result, the landscaping around the house took on a very "native" look—just pine trees and rocks. For one small area of the yard, we brought in three truckloads of dirt, put mulch on top of that and laid flagstone paths. But I didn't plant anything there. I knew the deer and bears

Lush flowers (left and below) surround the flagstone patio.

$ BUDGET SECRET: Give "volunteer" plants a chance to develop. They may be keepers. A plant that Ramona mistook for an oak—and almost pulled up—turned out to be a lovely celandine poppy.

would just eventually munch it away.

A BLANK CANVAS

But there was hope. The previous owners had turned the large side yard into a dog run and surrounded it with a 6-foot-high fence. This space contained nothing but ugly dirt, plus a few trees here and there. It was perfect for a deer-proof garden.

At least we thought it was perfect. Then we started trying to dig holes for planting.

Colorado clay doesn't even come close to the rich black soil of Illinois. There's a reason our neighborhood is called "Rockrimmon." With every shovelful, we unearthed nothing but rocks, from egg-sized lumps to small boulders. And what we dug up was unusable for planting, so we had to bring in new soil.

If we had it to do again, we would have skipped the digging and trucked in soil to make raised beds.

Still, we were fortunate. There were some natural assets within the enclosure, including a 40-foot pine tree, a shimmering aspen, a grove of small oak trees and a wonderful 4-foot by 2-foot boulder neatly located against the inside fence.

The first summer, we cleared weeds and laid out a design. Then Steve thought of a fish pond and decided to add a small water garden. Little did he know that after digging 6 inches down, he'd have to rent a jackhammer to punch through solid sandstone to finish the job.

We planted the basics that year—peonies, asters, rudbeckia and other hardy plants capable of withstanding the late snows and dry seasons of the High Plains. As a Midwestern native, I always thought snow meant moisture. But in the Front Range of the Rocky Mountains, the snow often evaporates in the dry air instead of melting into the ground.

BLOSSOMING LANDSCAPE

The next summer, I started trying the flowers I'd been dreaming about—roses, lilies and garden phlox. Although we're in Plant Hardiness Zone 5, there are pockets in the yard that are colder. And some years, it's like we're living in Zone 2! I spent a couple of years moving plants around and adding new ones to replace those flowers that froze in these cooler microclimates.

The existing oaks gave us an opportunity to try shade-loving plants like hostas that the deer would devour if planted outside the fence.

Columbine loves the dappled shade, as do bleeding heart, rubrum lily, astilbe, hellebore and lamium.

Gravel paths link the flower beds; below right, a charming gate opens onto the garden.

BUDGET SECRET:

You may not need to rent heavy machinery to move rocks around your yard. Slide flat rocks over metal pipes or round fence posts. To move rocks over grass, use a sled or rigid plastic swimming pool.

$

NATURE TAKES ROOT

As the garden matured, we were thrilled to see volunteer plants emerge. Fragrant Hyperion daylilies appeared one summer, and a low-growing purple dome aster spread like crazy. One plant I mistook for a wayward oak—and almost yanked out—turned out to be a celandine poppy. It gives us lovely yellow flowers every spring.

Birds must have dropped some hollyhock seeds, because we never planted any, but have a nice array of them against the fence.

We turned an empty corner of the enclosure into a seating area by laying a flagstone patio. We loved it so much that the next year we tripled its size, adding an area for a hammock where we can relax while watching the hummingbirds and bees enjoy what the deer would love to eat.

Deer did manage to come in a few times when I forgot to close the gate, however. They sure enjoyed the tulips!

I like to put in a few annuals each year, like cosmos, but most of the plants in the garden are perennials.

LESSONS LEARNED

To keep digging to a minimum, I use containers for anything that needs to be stored inside for winter, such as dahlias, angels' trumpets and gladiolas. That way, I just dump out the containers in fall, wrap up the tubers, and repot them the next year.

Now that I've figured out where everything should be, the perennials are doing well. The roses are thriving, thanks to the wood chips I place over them every fall for protection from the cold weather and the fish fertilizer I recycle from one of Steve's ponds.

To conserve moisture, we use lots of mulch, and we installed a drip irrigation system. This gives the roses a little extra moisture, and I water them by hand a couple times a month, too.

Now we have gravel paths dotted with flagstones that meander past two ponds. Our flower beds are bursting with scented charmers like phlox and sweet peas. And the entryway features a welcoming wrought-iron archway covered with Iceberg roses.

It's just like the garden in my dreams. 🌿

"Deer did come in a few times when I forgot to close the gate. They sure **enjoyed the tulips!**"

HERE'S THE
plan

1. Boulder
2. Hollyhock
3. Daylily
4. Perennials
5. Butterfly bush
6. Hosta
7. Oak
8. Patio
9. Honeysuckle vine
10. Primrose
11. Lilac
12. Phlox
13. Rose
14. Lily
15. Clematis
16. Pond
17. Aspen
18. Blackberry bush
19. Peony
20. Porcelain berry vine
21. Pine

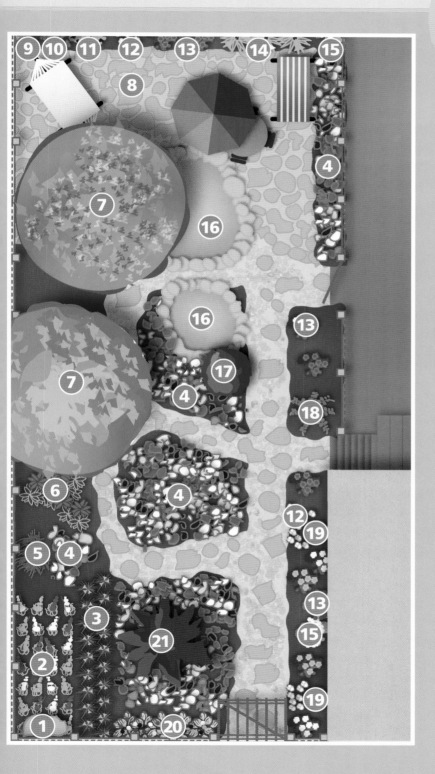

131

BETWEEN A rock & a hard place*

SUSAN PERREN
STAFFORD, VIRGINIA

SHE WENT TO EXTREMES TO CARVE OUT A GORGEOUS BACKYARD.

Through torrential rains, mudslides, and soil so hard it brought new meaning to "Earth's crust," Susan Perren learned a thing or two about extreme gardening.

She overcame all these obstacles on 3 wooded acres in Stafford, Virginia to create a refreshing, parklike landscape.

At her previous home, she won Lowe's All-American Lawn contest with a beautiful lawn on 1/4 acre. After winning that honor, Susan wanted more room to exercise her green thumb. So she uprooted to expand.

"We found this beautiful area where they cleared forest for homes," Susan says. "We knew the soil would need some work, but I didn't realize you couldn't get a shovel into the ground more than

a few inches before hitting rock."

Stubborn stones weren't enough to diminish this lifelong gardener's determination, though.

"Gardening has been a hobby of mine since I was 14 in 4-H," Susan says. "Each garden project I've taken on has gotten bigger and bigger, so I knew I just had to be patient."

OFF TO A QUICK START

Susan had little time to waste, though. She had four pickup truckloads of plant divisions from her old place that desperately needed to get into the ground. Otherwise, they'd die.

"I had compost and topsoil brought in, too," she says. "That's when I realized our lot was not graded properly. Every time it rained, our patio was covered with mud."

To fix that problem, Susan bought "castle blocks," which she hauled herself. She arranged the interlocking blocks to create two raised beds that hold in the soil. They're now the centerpieces of her well-sculpted backyard.

Once she had a place to hold flowers, Susan needed to find a way to work in the raised beds without tracking mud everywhere. She added gravel pathways, giving her easy access to her plants and a natural buffer when the clay soil can't absorb the rain.

"Because the yard is on a slope, I ended up designing it in layers," Susan explains. "The sod drains to the grav-

BUDGET SECRET:

$

For a low-cost solution to drainage problems, consider raised beds to hold the soil in place. Susan built hers with interlocking "castle blocks."

(in progress)

el paths, which drain to a dry creek that takes the water around the house. I haven't had trouble with mud and erosion since."

Because the dry creek crossed the walking paths, Susan built small arched bridges for a more natural look where the two intersect.

WORKING THE GREENS

Susan's final challenge was probably the most humbling. She attempted to produce a lush, green lawn like the one that earned her national recognition at her old house, only to strike out time and again.

"My first year, I didn't think I'd ever see grass," Susan says. "But I soon realized we needed to sod in front of the flower

> "Every time it rained, our patio was covered with **mud**."

beds because every time it rained the seed would wash into the gravel paths."

She seeded and reseeded the remainder of her yard several times with a sun/shade grass mix, creating a green carpet she's proud of.

Now that this extreme gardener has several victories over Mother Nature, what could possibly be left? Creating more flower beds, of course.

"I've worked hard on the lawn, but the way I figure, the more islands of flowers I have, the less grass I'll have to cut," Susan chuckles. ✤

Winding paths give Susan's yard a parklike feel.

HERE'S THE plan

1. Hosta
2. Daylily
3. Dry creek bed
4. Birdhouse/hollyhock garden
5. Arbor/fence
6. Perennial garden
7. Birdbath
8. Lilyturf
9. Bridge
10. Patio
11. Daffodils
12. Swing
13. Bird-feeding island
14. Butterfly garden
15. Arbor

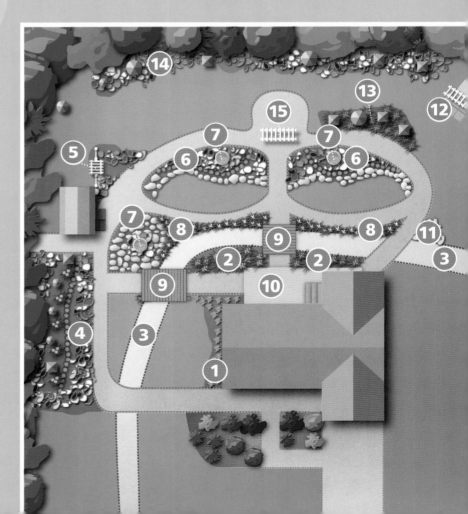

ANYTHING
but plains

THEY WORKED WITH THE WEATHER
TO KEEP TOUGH CONDITIONS FROM
BLOWING AWAY THE BACKYARD
OF THEIR DREAMS.

BY THERESA AND VERN BEILMAN
WICHITA, KANSAS

Sturdy fences are a must to protect the Beilmans' plants from harsh Kansas winds.

Mother Nature sure doesn't make it easy to garden in the Great Plains of Kansas. It can be 20° below in winter and 110° in summer…with watering restrictions. Then there's our infamous wind!

But in the past 30 years, husband Vern and I have learned how to work with the weather to create a backyard that makes us proud.

Much of our garden is made up of hand-me-down plants from neighbors and friends. This not only helped us save money while putting six children through college, it also meant the plants already were "Kansas tested." If they'd survived for other gardeners in our area, we figured they should work for us, too.

If there's one thing I've learned, it's not to mess with success—if it grows, leave it!

Given our harsh gardening conditions, plants recommended for full sun do well here

aged to grow azaleas by tucking them among the shelter of daylilies on the north side of the house. And our Japanese maple has thrived, while other gardeners have seen theirs struggle.

I start planting as early as February, protecting young starts at night with plastic sheets draped over stakes and anchored with rocks.

Vern also built a cold frame (bottom left). He's a master at nurturing seedlings, so many plants get a head start in this mini greenhouse.

One thing we've found is that sturdy wooden or stone fences are an absolute necessity. These offer some wind protection, especially for tall perennials.

Still, there are many times we can't protect our flowers. One year we lost most of our columbines after a storm covered the entire garden with 3 inches of solid ice. A 'Nelly Moser' clematis is my pride and joy, but we know one

"If there's **one thing I've learned,** it's

in partial shade. Hardy lilies grow beautifully, as do purple coneflowers, phlox, bee balm, cannas and annuals like zinnias, marigolds, morning glories and moss roses. I fill shady areas with columbine, hostas and foxgloves.

Irises are a trusty standby in Kansas, offering striking blooms in early summer and nice foliage for the rest of the growing season.

A couple plants have surprised us. I man-

severe winter or summer could wipe it out.

In addition to the harsh weather, we also face extremely dry summers. We water judiciously and select plants and lawn grasses—like zoysia—that can tolerate a little drought.

We use a lot of homemade mulch, leaves and lawn clippings to enrich the flower beds. The soil is hard-packed clay, so it really benefits from this added organic material. We have a

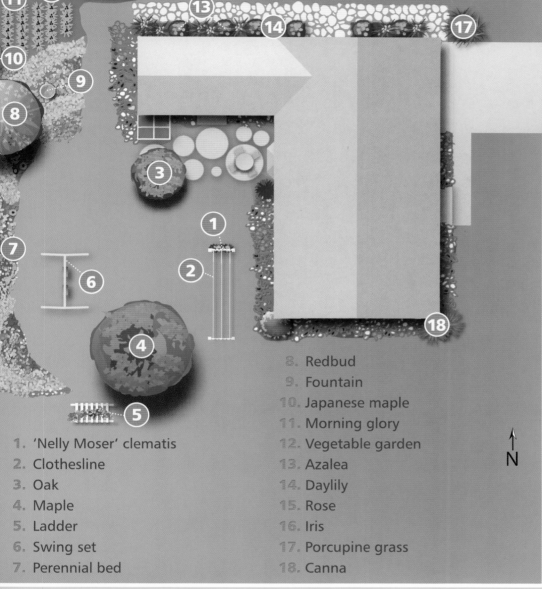

1. 'Nelly Moser' clematis
2. Clothesline
3. Oak
4. Maple
5. Ladder
6. Swing set
7. Perennial bed
8. Redbud
9. Fountain
10. Japanese maple
11. Morning glory
12. Vegetable garden
13. Azalea
14. Daylily
15. Rose
16. Iris
17. Porcupine grass
18. Canna

N

not to mess with success. If it grows, leave it!"

large compost area we've disguised by planting morning glories on a lattice in front of it.

I've tried to create several private spots in our small garden. One gravel path leads to a bench, fountain and planter boxes beneath a redbud tree. It's a favorite place for us to sit with our grandchildren and cool off.

Even when our grandchildren aren't visiting, there are reminders of them—and our children—everywhere in the garden. A ladder propped against the maple tree once served our boys' tree house. Now I use it to display potted geraniums, anchored to the rungs with nails through the drainage holes.

Gardening in this part of Kansas isn't exactly a breeze, but we've discovered lots of low-cost tricks and techniques to breathe life into our little plot.

TAKING ON A
mountain

BY RENAE AND BOBBY RHODES
CHITTENDEN, VERMONT

THEY TAMED THEIR BACKYARD
BY SHOWERING IT WITH FLOWERS.

Our backyard may look like a paradise, but getting it to look like this was quite a challenge. This particular backyard is on a mountain!

The yard is filled with rocks and plenty of slate. In this part of Vermont, it's rare to hit "real dirt." But my husband, Bobby, and I found ways to make do with what we had.

A BLOOMING ALTERNATIVE

We began gardening out of necessity. If you've ever tried to mow the lawn on the side of a mountain, you soon learn that flowers are an easier (and prettier) alternative. So we began adding flower beds in some of the areas that were the most difficult to mow.

Bobby was the one with vision, finding places for new gardens that I never dreamed of. He's a jeweler and likes to work with his hands. He built, hauled or designed almost everything on our property, while I took care of maintenance, planting and dividing.

When we first started landscaping, our collection of plants quickly grew because it seemed that I stopped at every nursery we passed.

Often, we'd load up our truck with new plants, and then return home to create new gardens to put them in. The beds began multiplying, creating a colorful stairway down the mountain.

Bobby also brought a bit of his Southern heritage to our yard. He's from South Carolina, a state known for its beautiful gardens.

Whenever we visited relatives, we stopped at many of the mansions and plantations in the area. Their gardens gave us some ideas for our backyard (like the magnolia we added) and something to strive for.

And just for fun, we extended that Southern feel by naming many of our gardens after places mentioned in my favorite movie, *Gone with the Wind*.

But unlike much of the South, we have rocky soil. This takes a lot of hard work. Luckily, Bobby has plenty of energy. He works manure and peat moss in to create soil that's loose enough for me to plant perennials.

BUDGET SECRET:

$

Renae divides perennials as they spread. This not only saves cash but provides continuity for large spaces.

Dense plantings help control weeds in this sloping yard.

Renae and Bobby chose hardy plants for their gardens, which spill down the side of a mountain (below).

"Gardeners are always willing to share **new things** or pass on a start or two."

I chose only hardy plants and shrubs that would stand up to some pretty tough conditions (including hungry deer). I've planted lots of perennials that spread year after year even in our difficult soil. Some of my favorites are hostas for the shady areas, irises, daylilies, sedums and ground covers.

We also added some beautiful flowering shrubs, including azaleas, daphne, potentilla, lilacs and weigela.

Barberry is one of my favorite shrubs. Its deep burgundy color and rich texture make a pretty backdrop for other plants.

As plants began to spread, I divided them and moved starts into other beds. That saved a lot of money and provided continuity throughout the gardens.

GENEROUS GREEN THUMBS

Bobby and I learned what we know about gardening from books, experience and, most of all, other helpful gardeners.

That's one thing that's impressed me about gardeners—they're always willing to share new things or pass on a start or two. I was always excited when people did this for us. I started doing this, too, inviting people who walked up our driveway for a glimpse to come in for a closer look.

Many people have asked how we maintain a yard this large without help from a gardener. I simply tell them, "Mulch." This helps keep the weeds down, plus it looks nice.

Our beds have filled in nicely, although I don't think the gardens will ever be "done." When you're taming a mountain, victories come a little at a time. 🌿

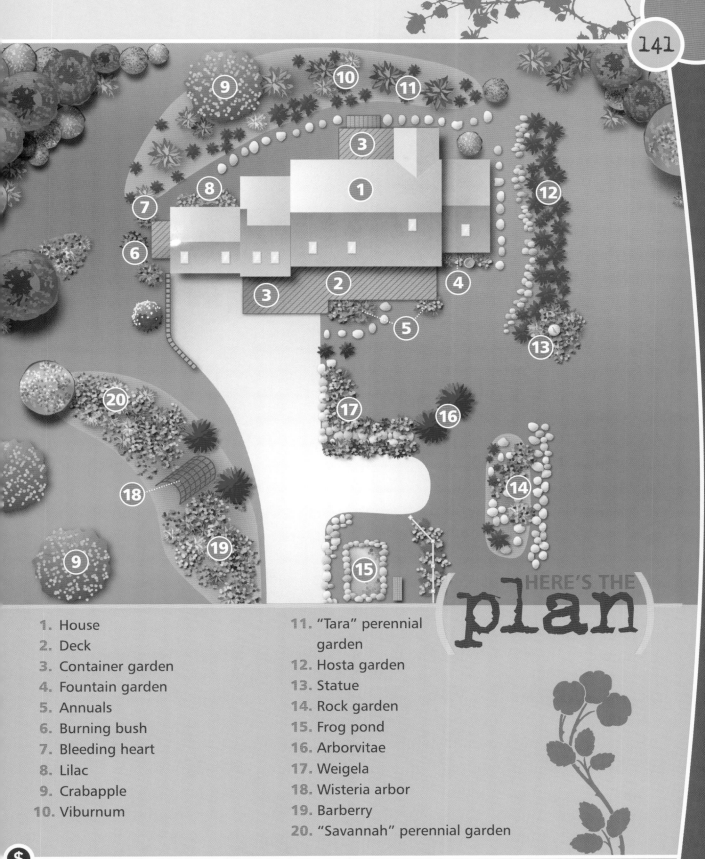

HERE'S THE (plan)

1. House
2. Deck
3. Container garden
4. Fountain garden
5. Annuals
6. Burning bush
7. Bleeding heart
8. Lilac
9. Crabapple
10. Viburnum
11. "Tara" perennial garden
12. Hosta garden
13. Statue
14. Rock garden
15. Frog pond
16. Arborvitae
17. Weigela
18. Wisteria arbor
19. Barberry
20. "Savannah" perennial garden

$ **BUDGET SECRET:** Renae divides perennials as they spread. This saves money, but it also provides continuity, especially for large areas.

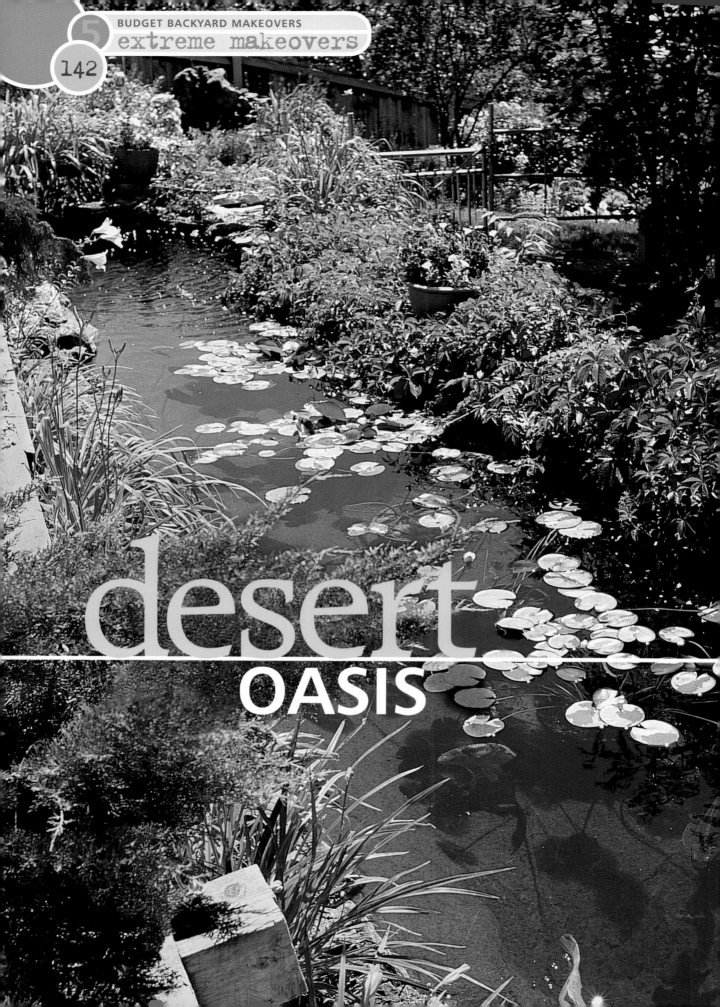

desert
OASIS

THEIR ONCE-ARID BACKYARD IS NOW A LUSH LANDSCAPE.

**BY SUSAN AND BILL MOYER
GRAND JUNCTION, COLORADO**

Knee-high weeds, rock-hard dirt and some half-dead aspens—that's all the backyard this property in Grand Junction, Colorado had to offer when my husband, Bill, bought it just before we married in 1996.

Bill's first backyard projects were nothing to write home about, just a lot of hard work. He mainly pulled weeds and coaxed grass to grow where there was none.

Then there was the impossible soil, which consisted primarily of adobe and bentonite clay. Mix in a high mountain desert climate and a less-than-ideal steep hillside location, and Bill was brewing a recipe for a garden disaster.

Undaunted by these obstacles— and not fully realizing how poor the soil was—I joined his efforts. We started planting perennial beds and adding shrubs and trees, only to watch the plants struggle to survive. It took two full growing seasons of disappointments before we got a clue. We needed to talk to other, more experienced gardeners before we put another plant into this landscape.

We chatted with neighboring gardeners, stopped the staff at nearby nurseries, read everything we could find on gardening in our climate and attended several garden tours. Our research began to lead us down the proper path.

"Soil amendment," everyone kept repeating. And we picked up on one more common suggestion…mulch heavily to retain moisture, especially during blazing hot summer weather.

We consider this the true starting point of our backyard makeover. We worked a ton of sheep manure and peat into the unforgiving soil, added fertilizer and topped it all off with a truckload of mulch. Things began to change for the better. Today, our yard resembles

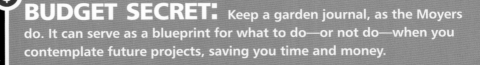

$ BUDGET SECRET: Keep a garden journal, as the Moyers do. It can serve as a blueprint for what to do—or not do—when you contemplate future projects, saving you time and money.

"Bill dug every inch of the

(in progress)

the kind of lush garden you'd see in a kinder, more plant-friendly area. In this area, it sticks out like a thumb—a green one!

STEADY STREAM OF IDEAS

The biggest addition was Bill's remarkable cascading stream and waterfalls. They dance down from the top of our backyard to our deck, which hangs over the water. It's the focal point of the backyard, taking full advantage of the steep slope our house is built on.

Bill dug every inch of the pond and stream. It measures 12 feet wide and 35 feet long. He also hauled in and placed each rock along the waterway, as well as those he used to create paths, benches and two other smaller water gardens.

All three water features are filled with water lilies, cattails, bog beans, water cannas, hyacinths and other plants.

Flower beds surround the entire lot. In spring, daffodils, crocuses and tulips burst with brilliance. Come summer, roses, daylilies, irises, trumpet vines, calendula, dahlias, poppies and other perennials take over. In fall, we make room for chrysanthemums. I think we've plant-

BUDGET SECRET: Tough growing conditions? Don't waste money on fragile flowers. Ask neighbors to recommend their favorite can't-miss plants. **$**

A path and flower beds create soothing views; top right, Bill tends to water plants.

ed more than 100 different perennials so far.

Although the beds brim with flowers, we learned to be choosy. Only plants that tolerate poor soil, low humidity and extreme heat survive in our yard. More tender species, like azaleas, were spectacular failures, and pansies faded quickly in the heat. We learned to admire these beauties, along with dozens of others that didn't make it, in magazines and books instead.

PACKED WITH SHRUBS AND TREES

To round out our landscape, we scattered flowering shrubs and ornamental trees throughout the yard, like flowering quince, weeping mulberry, bluebeard, butterfly bushes and cherry, plum and apricot trees.

We've also had good luck experimenting with trees that don't typically belong in this climate. We gave yellow groove bamboo a try about 9 years ago and now have a robust grove that soars above our house, much to everyone's amazement. (Note: Before planting anything uncommon to your area, make sure it won't become invasive or weedy.)

Bill's pride and joy is a towering weeping false cypress near the pond. The tree is native to the Northwest, but it's doing well in our desert area and has more than doubled its size in a few short years.

One of the most interesting discoveries in the yard occurred when we expanded the perennial beds in our side yard. Bill unearthed a huge odd-shaped rock that looked like a di-

1. Koi pond
2. Perennials
3. Aspen
4. Weeping false cypress
5. Stone footbridge
6. Chitalpa tree
7. Weeping cherry
8. Stone bench
9. Mulberry
10. Amur chokecherry
11. Meditation pond
12. Bluebeard
13. 'Purple Crown' locust
14. Dinosaur Garden
15. Butterfly bush
16. Apricot
17. Spruce
18. Pyracantha
19. Iris
20. Rose-of-Sharon
21. Rock garden
22. Rose bed
23. Shed
24. Bamboo
25. Weeping mulberry
26. Flowering quince
27. 'Mt. Fuji' flowering cherry
28. Flowering plum

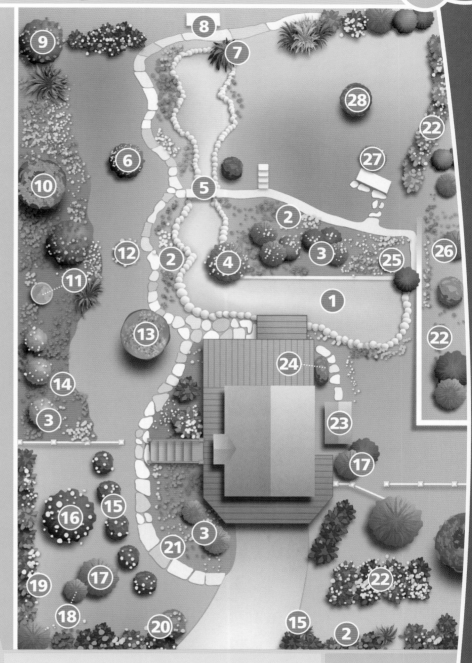

HERE'S THE
plan

nosaur footprint. A local paleontologist said the rock was a casting of a footprint left by a hadrosaur, an 18- to 20-foot-tall duck-billed herbivore. The rock weighs more than 60 pounds and is proudly displayed on our deck. Of course, we now call the perennial bed the Dinosaur Garden.

The Western Colorado Botanical Society has featured our yard on a garden tour. More than 500 people wandered the paths along our stream and pond, and strolled among the flowers. That was a real thrill, but we're not quite finished yet. Bill and I think of the yard as a work in progress. But it's nice to sit back on the deck now and then and enjoy what we've accomplished. ❦

beauty
AND THE
beach

THE LAKE VIEW WAS ALREADY GREAT. HARD WORK MADE IT SPECTACULAR.

**TOM AND MARY BECKER
ROGERS CITY, MICHIGAN**

Count Tom and Mary Becker lucky. Lake Huron is the first thing they look at every day, and it's an incredible view. Even more incredible, they found a way to improve it!

"The land was untouched when we bought it," Mary says from their home in Rogers City, Michigan. "No one had ever built anything on this property. There was nothing here but woods."

The Beckers built a home in 1989 and created a small lawn, but left the untamed area between the house and the beach untouched.

"We lived with the 'wild' look for several years," Mary recalls. "We considered just leaving it natural, but we both wanted something a little more groomed, incorporating our house into the landscape. So we decided to clear some of the area."

BREAKING A SWEAT

But as they quickly discovered, that was easier said than done. The property was covered with wild cedar shrubs.

"The roots go on forever and the plants were all interconnected," Mary says. "It took us a whole season to pull the cedar out and have a place to start working."

While pulling out the underbrush, they uncovered a depression Mary calls "a semi-ravine."

"We didn't know what we were going to do with it, until we came up with the idea for a pond," she says. "But we had so much debris falling out of our trees that we decided not to fill it with water. Instead, we created a dry creek bed and dry pond.

"The two of us hand-picked the rocks at a quarry and built the pond and stream ourselves."

Tom and Mary also created a walkway of paver bricks and two stepping-stone paths, one running along the dry creek bed and the other leading to the beach.

With the yard's framework in place, they were ready to plant the gardens they'd sketched on paper. There was just one problem—no soil.

"All we had was sand under a layer of soft, spongy moss and decayed leaves," Mary says. "It was mushy when you walked across it, with an earthy aroma."

A county Extension agent suggested the Beckers visit a nearby cranberry bog to obtain peat for a soil amendment. They mixed the peat

Rustic log benches surround the fire pit.

HERE'S THE plan

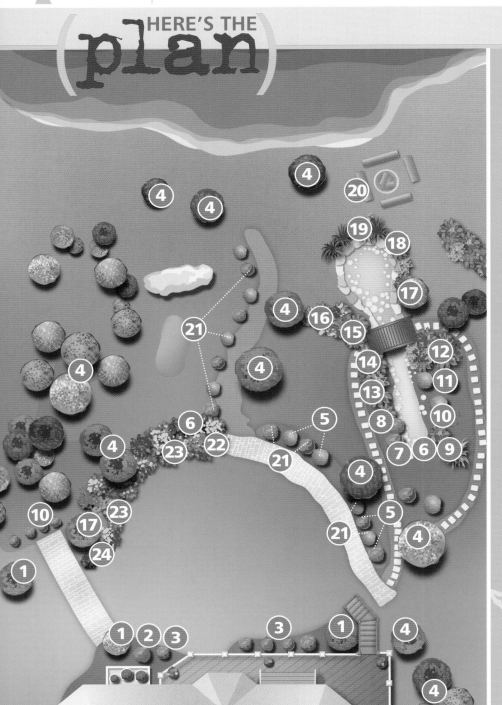

1. Crabapple
2. Cotoneaster
3. Barberry
4. Pine
5. Hosta
6. 'Autumn Joy' sedum
7. 'Moonbeam' coreopsis
8. Silvermound artemisia
9. Daylily
10. Currant bush
11. Rhubarb
12. Raspberries
13. Lavender
14. Blue sage
15. English ivy
16. Moss rose
17. Birch
18. Burning bush
19. Ornamental grasses
20. Fire pit
21. Yew
22. Peony
23. Melampodium
24. Hydrangea

with dirt they had delivered, and added some clay so the soil would hold moisture. They built berms for gardens, but amended the soil only in selected areas. They wanted to leave most of the land natural.

HARSH ELEMENTS

Even with amended soil and raised beds, the Beckers had a hard time finding plants that would tolerate shade, wind, and northern Michigan's abbreviated growing season.

"We used trial and error the first few years," Mary says. "Tom really wanted roses, but after several years of unsatisfactory results, he gave up. The cold wind blowing off the lake is the culprit. We've found that evergreens perform best, so we keep adding new ones."

The Beckers also rely on hardy perennials, like hostas and 'Autumn Joy' sedum, that can take all that their climate dishes out.

"Hostas and evergreens are foolproof," Mary says. "They're just no-brainers."

FAMILY GATHERING PLACE

The Beckers did all the work themselves, but their sons and sons-in-law helped Tom fash-ion rustic log benches around the fire pit.

"We considered that a family project, built for all of us to enjoy," Mary says. "We have 10 children and 2 dozen grandchildren. All of them live far away, but they come every year and have a big bonfire. That's a big thing with us."

Tom and Mary also installed wooden steps near the fire pit for easier beach access.

"A neighbor had removed a tree and cut it in-to slabs so the pieces could be moved," Mary says. "Lots of sweat went into that project. We could hardly get the wheelbarrow through the sand, so we pulled some of them down the slope on a sled. That was an aching-back day…let's say week!

"It looks even better now that the wind has blown sand around the steps."

When all's quiet, there's nothing more satis-fying to Tom and Mary than sitting on their deck, soaking in the picture-perfect lake view.

Lucky? Maybe. But you need more than luck to take a scene only nature can provide…and improve it. ❧

The Beckers hand-picked rocks for their dry creek bed.

BUDGET SECRET:

$ When a tree falls, use it. The Beckers turned one downed tree into benches for the fire pit, and used another to create steps leading from the fire pit down to the beach.

"Hostas and **evergreens are foolproof.** They're just no-brainers."

BRIGHTideas

BOLD AND BEAUTIFUL

Extreme conditions call for creative solutions. These real-life solutions produced beauty in less-than-perfect environments.

a desert oasis Budget-savvy water conservation helped create this lush backyard—in a region that gets less than 11 inches of water a year. Shelley Grossman of Carlsbad, California collects water in rain barrels and irrigates her garden with water diverted from her washing machine and shower, with storage for any excess. This system works so well that Shelley has enough water left over to fill a small swimming pool and pond for several months of the year.

the root of the problem Exposed tree roots weren't just an eyesore in Pat Miller's Piscataway, New Jersey yard—they were a hazard. Some of the roots extended 4 inches above the soil, along the route everyone took to the pool and garden. "I found the arched bridges in a closeout catalog and got them for a song, and my husband put them together," Pat says. "Then I added impatiens and ground covers to create the illusion of a continuous stream of flowers. All told, we spent less than $65 to solve this pesky problem."

sun and shade When drought and watering restrictions decimated Dick Rosenquist's backyard in Saratoga, California, he installed his own irrigation system and then built this stunning pavilion. The airy latticework design creates a cool, soothing look in addition to dappled shade. Dick also added a pond, complete with a low-cost filtration system made from a water trough from the local feed store.

rock-bottom bargain A sandstone deposit unearthed during excavation for a new basement left Mark and Mary Williamson with 60 tons of boulders in their yard. The Montezuma, Indiana couple saved a bundle on landscaping by using the rocks for paths, garden borders, a dry creek bed and more. "The stream bed didn't cost us a dime, but diverts rainfall just as well as a professionally installed retaining wall or under-the-driveway culvert," Mary says.

TOUGH CONDITIONS?
THESE PLANTS CAN TAKE IT!

BLANKET FLOWER
GAILLARDIA X GRANDIFLORA

Bloom time: All summer.

Light needs: Full sun.

Hardiness: Zones 3 to 9.

Mature plant size: 2 to 3 feet high, 1 to 2 feet wide.

Care tip: Light, well-drained soil is important (it will falter in clay). You can start seed indoors early.

RUGOSA ROSE
ROSA RUGOSA AND CULTIVARS

Bloom time: Late spring through fall.

Light needs: Full sun.

Hardiness: Zones 2 to 7 or 8.

Mature plant size: 4 to 8 feet high and wide.

Care tip: Do not use chemical sprays; fortunately, it's much more pest- and disease-resistant than other types of roses.

SEDUM
SEDUM SPECIES AND CULTIVARS

Bloom time: Midsummer through fall.

Light needs: Full to partial sun.

Hardiness: Zones 4 to 8 or 9.

Mature plant size: 1 to 2 feet high and wide.

Care tip: Self-sufficient in average soil and full sun.

LILYTURF
LIRIOPE MUSCARI

Bloom time: Spring to summer.

Light needs: Full sun to partial shade.

Hardiness: Zones 4 to 10.

Mature plant size: 8 to 12 inches high and spreading.

Care tip: Remove or mow down old foliage every spring to make way for fresh new growth.

YARROW
ACHILLEA SPECIES AND CULTIVARS

Bloom time: Summer.

Light needs: Full sun.

Hardiness: Zones 4 to 8.

Mature plant size: 1 to 3 feet high, 1 foot wide.

Care tip: Actually forms a stronger plant and blooms better in lean soil; performs best in full sun.

DIFFICULT GROWING CONDITIONS CAN DAMPEN A GARDENER'S DREAMS. BUT A SURPRISING ARRAY OF PLANTS ADAPT TO ALMOST ANYTHING NATURE CAN DISH OUT. THESE SURVIVORS ARE GREAT CHOICES FOR TOUGH CONDITIONS.

BLUE OAT GRASS
HELICHTOTRICHON SEMPERVIRENS

Bloom time: Early summer.

Light needs: Full sun.

Hardiness: Zones 5 to 8.

Mature plant size: 1 to 2 feet high and wide.

Care tip: For best foliage color, give it full sun in cooler regions, light shade in warmer areas.

ICELAND POPPY
PAPAVER NUDICALE

Bloom time: Spring to summer.

Light needs: Full sun to partial shade.

Hardiness: Zones 2 to 7.

Mature plant size: 12 to 18 inches high, 12 inches wide.

Care tip: Runs out of steam after two or three great seasons, so plan to replace with more.

PEONY
PAEONIA HYBRIDS

Bloom time: Spring.

Light needs: Full to partial sun.

Hardiness: Zones 3 to 8.

Mature plant size: Up to 3 feet high and wide.

Care tip: Too much shade reduces flowering. Plant shallowly (1 to 2 inches deep) in fertile soil.

SERVICEBERRY, JUNEBERRY
AMELANCHIER SPECIES AND CULTIVARS

Bloom time: Late spring.

Light needs: Full sun to partial shade.

Hardiness: Zones 5 to 9.

Mature plant size: Varies; some are up to 20 feet tall and wide.

Care tip: Makes a fine informal hedge or windbreak.

BLAZING STAR
LIATRIS SPECIES AND CULTIVARS

Bloom time: Summer.

Light needs: Full to partial sun.

Hardiness: Zones 3 to 9.

Mature plant size: 2 to 5 feet high, 1 to 2 feet wide.

Care tip: Once established, its tuberous rootstock will anchor it and enable it to survive drought amazingly well.

worth its weight in
BLACK GOLD

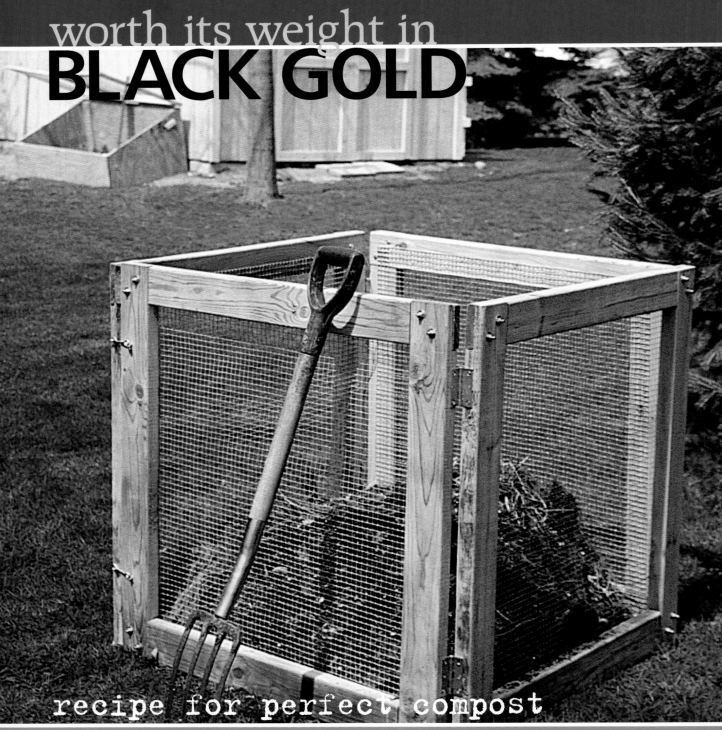

recipe for perfect compost

GREENS/WET
Fruit waste, eggshells, coffee grounds, vegetable waste, weeds (without seed heads), grass clippings, manure, seaweed

BROWNS/DRY
Newspaper, sawdust, most tree leaves, wood chips, cornstalks and cobs, straw and hay

COMPOST NO-NOS
Dairy products, animal waste, diseased or insect-infested plants, animal products (including bones and skin), egg whites and yolks, chemical-treated plants, oils or oily food scraps

THIS COMPOST BIN LETS YOU JUMP IN WITH BOTH FEET!

If your yard needs an extreme makeover, improve the soil first. This sounds tough, but compost makes it easy. It's the ultimate soil amendment—experienced gardeners call it "black gold." And you can make it for free! All it takes is a blend of yard and kitchen waste.

Unlike sprawling compost piles, this bin keeps the contents neatly contained. Air can circulate freely, which is essential for breaking down the ingredients, and the bin opens on any side, so it's super-easy to turn the pile.

Put your bin in a level, well-drained area in full sun, with good air circulation. Add equal parts brown and green wastes (see list of ingredients on page 152). To aerate the pile, mix or toss frequently with a garden fork, or poke air holes into it with a broom handle. Keep the pile moist, like a sponge, but not soaking wet.

The process is finished when the bottom of the pile has dark, rich soil that crumbles in your hand. 🌿

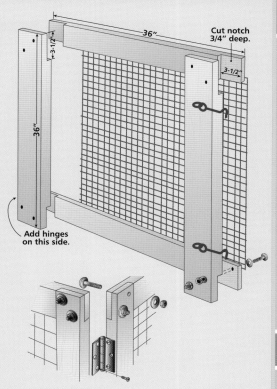

36"

Cut notch 3/4" deep.

3-1/2"

3-1/2"

36"

Add hinges on this side.

WHAT YOU NEED:

- Eight pressure-treated 6-foot 2 x 4's
- Thirty-two 5/16-inch x 2-inch carriage bolts, nuts and washers
- Four 3-inch door hinges
- Four large hook-and-eye assemblies
- 12-foot x 36-inch hardware cloth, 1/2-inch squares
- Poultry wire staples
- Waterproof construction adhesive

RECOMMENDED TOOLS:

- Table or circular saw
- Rafter square
- Power drill
- Chisel
- Rasp
- Tin snips
- Pliers
- Heavy-duty work gloves

BUILD YOUR OWN BIN

1. Cut each 2 x 4 in half to make 16 3-foot pieces.

2. Cut a 3-1/2-inch x 3/4-inch deep notch (a rabbet) in both ends of each piece. You can do this on a table saw or with a circular saw. Make several close cuts (about 1/8 inch apart) across the grain in the notched section. Use a hammer and chisel to break out the wood between these cuts. Smooth with a rasp.

3. Fit notched ends together to make four 3-foot-square frames. Drill holes for two carriage bolts in opposite corners of each notch (see illustrations above). Use construction adhesive in each joint before assembling. The nuts should face the outside so the bolts won't catch on your clothes when you're turning the pile.

4. Use tin snips to cut the hardware cloth into four 3-foot-square sections.

5. Tack each corner of the hardware cloth to the frame with poultry wire staples. Then staple around the frame every 2 inches.

6. Connect two frames with two door hinges, then put two hook-and-eye gate latches on the other ends. Repeat this step for the remaining two frames.

7. Stand the frames to form a square and latch the sections together. Then fill 'er up!

heaven
on earth

6

"PUTTERING AROUND" TAKES ON NEW MEANING IN THIS SUBURBAN BACKYARD.

STEVE AND CHRIS LISTER
GREENDALE, WISCONSIN

Steve and Chris Lister's tranquil little house doesn't stand out from other homes lining their quaint, historic street in Greendale, Wisconsin. Sure, their doorstep plantings are pretty. But it isn't until you step around back that you realize their parklike half-acre backyard is like no other in this quiet Milwaukee suburb.

The sprawling setting, created over the last 14 years, surprises most visitors. It's filled with an abundance of flowers, foliage and trees, benches for relaxing, a fire pit, a graceful gazebo…even a putting green.

"My son and I are avid golfers," Steve says. "We thought it would be a great idea to add the putting green so we could practice whenever we wanted."

That's just one of the charming features that make this backyard landscape extraordinary.

When the Listers bought the place, the landscape consisted of grass and some old cottonwoods that had to be removed. Their first effort—installing a few burning bushes—was modest compared to what followed.

"We were pretty green at gardening," Steve recalls. "We ended up moving the bushes because we didn't like where we planted them. Those shrubs migrated around the lot until we eventually found the perfect location."

MARITAL MOTIVATION

The Listers' landscaping ambitions kicked into high gear in 1994, when their son decided he and his fiancee would tie the knot in the backyard. Steve, a carpenter by trade, built a cedar gazebo to showcase the wedding cake and gifts.

"We also installed underground wiring and water lines and planted white flowers all around," says Chris. "We were busy working and decorating right up until the wedding.

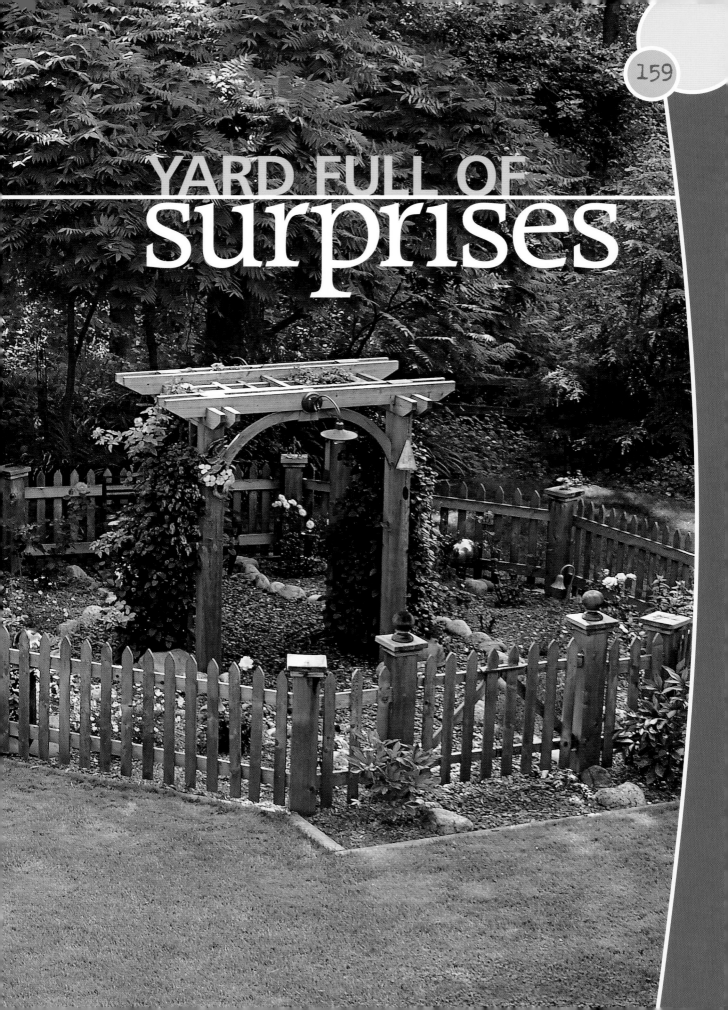

YARD FULL OF
surprises

The day before, Steve was still scrambling to get the gazebo's stairs built!

"It was all worth it, though," he says. "The day was perfect and we were fortunate to be able to celebrate this important event with 300 guests in our own backyard."

It was such a success that Steve's brother called about his own upcoming nuptials.

"When I asked him where he was going to get married, my brother said, 'Your backyard, of course,'" Steve recalls. "We've since had total strangers knock on our door to ask if they could hold their wedding out back."

This inspired the Listers to keep creating new features, like a pergola and arbor, which give the sprawling backyard some structure.

"Steve never drew up plans for any of the projects he's built," Chris says. "He just pictures what he wants to make and then gets out his tools and does it."

SIT A SPELL

Steve made several benches for the backyard, so visitors can relax and enjoy the view, which includes a creek that meanders alongside.

"As we worked in different parts of the yard, we'd notice that there wasn't a convenient place to sit," Steve says. "So we'd say to each other, 'Well, it looks like we need to put another bench here.' That's why there are benches scattered all over."

The wooden deck and stone patio adjacent to the house are also great vantage points.

SPECIAL PLANTINGS

The Listers love flowers and lower-growing greenery. Planters adorn the deck, and the yard includes several separate gardens. They also created a fenced-in rose garden as a tribute to Steve's grandparents, planting a pair of rosebushes on what would have been their 74th wedding anniversary.

"It was a wonderful tribute," Steve says. "Grandma just loved roses."

The yard's a popular attraction whenever the neighborhood hosts a public garden walk, but the Listers say it's far from finished.

"We constantly get new ideas when we see other gardens or look through magazines," Steve says. "And it isn't unusual for us to move established plants to make room for new ones.

"In fact, as soon as I think we're done, we find ourselves back at the nursery. It's definitely a yard in progress. That's the fun of it!" 🌿

The Listers' yard features a putting green, plus a fire pit (left).

BUDGET SECRET: Don't have time or money to maintain a picture-perfect putting green? Steve doesn't, either. His secret? Artificial turf.

$

HERE'S THE
plan

1. American flag
2. Japanese maple
3. Hazelnut
4. Weeping pussy willow
5. Tomatoes
6. Annuals
7. Honey locust
8. Hosta
9. Gazebo
10. 'Crimson King' Norway maple
11. Red cedar
12. Burning bush
13. Fire pit
14. Weeping cherry
15. Peony
16. Conifers
17. Memorial rose garden
18. Putting green
19. Sand trap
20. Shed
21. Picnic area
22. Pergola

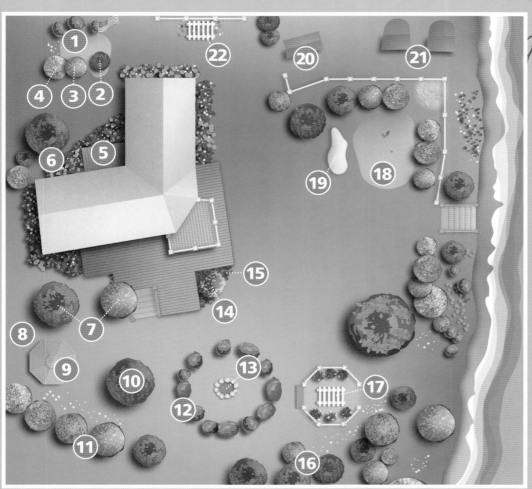

making HER mark

JIM AND JUDY SHUGART
LAKE CHARLES, LOUISIANA

THIS GARDENER BLOOMS WHEREVER SHE'S PLANTED.

"I don't like yards with blank spaces," Louisiana gardener Judy Shugart says. "If I see a spot that lacks color or character, I do my best to fill it in by planting shrubs and trees and adding flower beds."

She's had lots of practice. She and her husband, Jim, have relocated five times since they married. She's landscaped around each house herself.

"When we moved into our home in Lafayette, the yard was basically bare," Judy says. "That gave me all the motivation I needed to start gardening."

She began slowly, focusing on one corner of the yard, then another.

"If I thought about everything I wanted to do, I felt overwhelmed," she says. "So I concentrated on a single task at a time, like adding azaleas around the house."

To spread out the bloom time for these flowering shrubs, Judy consulted experts at the local garden center and chose several azalea varieties so they'd bloom at different times.

"They start to blossom as soon as our rainy, cold winters are over," she says. "It's such a treat to see them burst into color."

Soon, other shrubs and flowering trees began to dot the landscape, including camellia, gardenia,

BUDGET SECRET:

Don't go to the effort and expense of removing a stump. Just landscape around it. Judy surrounded a stump with variegated privet and Texas sage, then filled in with pots of flowers.

rose-of-Sharon, bridal wreath, crape myrtle, holly and big-leaf magnolia.

"I chose the camellias because they begin to bud in early January," Judy says. "That's one of the things I love about living in the Deep South—I can count on flowers to brighten things up almost any time of year."

As the gardens grew, Judy and Jim made their share of errors.

"We did everything from putting shade-loving plants in sunny spots to choosing varieties that are better suited for other climates," Judy says. "But each mistake was a lesson, too."

PERSONAL TOUCHES

Along the way, Jim and Judy also added stone walkways that meander around the backyard and created a whimsical playhouse that also serves as a hothouse.

Varied flowers, such as snapdragons and violas in spring and begonias and vinca in summer, add splashes of color. The grassy foliage of lily-

Graceful lilyturf and container plants add charm to Judy's garden.

raise and lower actual flower beds," she says.

Containers of pansies, violas, daffodils, dwarf snapdragons and corn lilies also provided instant beauty when the Shugarts had to remove a mature tree.

The Shugarts have had **five different homes,** and Judy's done the landscaping at all of them.

---

turf lines the paths, and assorted birdbaths, feeders and birdhouses attract winged friends to the yard.

Most of Judy's flowers won't be found in the ground, however.

"I've taken to container gardening in a big way," she says. "I have back trouble, so bending and kneeling in the garden was too painful. I switched my focus to planters, knowing I could sit at a table to put them together."

Judy found another advantage to planting in containers.

"It's a lot easier to vary the height of different pots by setting some on bricks than it is to

"I knew that spot could become an interesting garden, so we left the stump and surrounded it with variegated privet and Texas sage," Judy says. "Then I filled in the space with pots of flowers. It was instantly pretty."

After all their hard work, leaving wasn't easy.

"We had to move because of Jim's job," Judy says. "We felt sad about having to say good-bye to these gardens that we'd put our heart and soul into."

IN GOOD HANDS

Understandably, it was important that they find the right person to care for the yard, and they did—another avid gardener.

"We loved her right away," Judy says. "We now make frequent visits to see her and the gardens."

Between trips, Judy's busy recreating old gardens at her new home in Lake Charles, 75 miles west of Lafayette.

"It's going to be a while before this yard will look as pretty as the one we fixed up in Lafayette," Judy says. "But I know that in the not-too-distant future, Jim and I will be able to enjoy a cup of coffee in another beautiful setting we've built ourselves." ❧

HERE'S THE
plan

1. Variegated privet
2. Snapdragon
3. Pansy
4. Chrysanthemum
5. Tree stump
6. Birdbath
7. Flowerpot
8. Camellia
9. Crape myrtle
10. Gardenia
11. Rose-of-Sharon

12. Oak tree
13. Banana plant
14. Lilyturf
15. Azalea
16. Red tip photinia
17. Holly tree
18. Wheelbarrow planter
19. Bridal wreath
20. Playhouse
21. Bigleaf magnolia

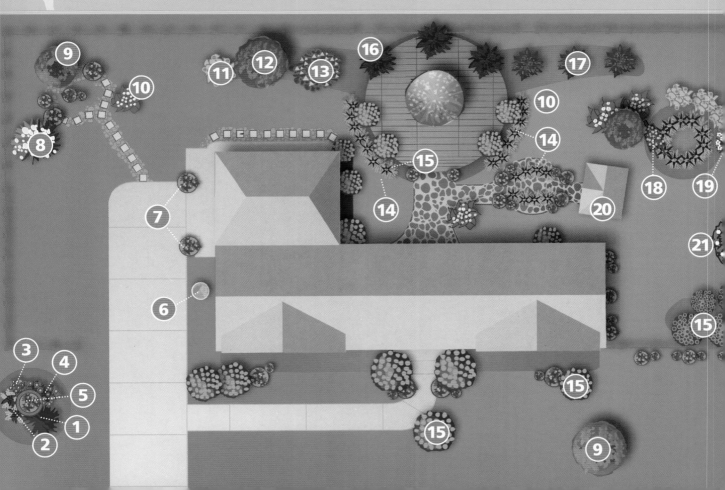

rising
TO THE
challenge

NEW SURROUNDINGS AND A HELPFUL NEIGHBOR SPURRED THEIR GARDENING ASPIRATIONS.

BY NITA AND DAVE ASTON
LEWISTON, IDAHO

Our gardening adventure began more than 20 years ago, when our family moved from Southern California to the beautiful, but wetter and cooler, state of Idaho.

It was late winter when we arrived. We didn't expect a yard ablaze with colorful flowers, but hoped spring would uncover little purple crocuses, yellow daffodils or pink tulips. Alas, it didn't happen.

However, our backyard did yield one rather large plant that a knowledgeable neighbor identified as rhubarb. We certainly had a lot to learn about gardening.

LITTLE SPROUTS

Seeing our disappointment with the backyard's condition, our gardening neighbor began sharing her wisdom—and her plants—with us. At the time, it seemed impossible to make our yard look as lovely as hers, but we accepted the challenge.

During our first few years in Idaho, my husband, Dave, and I were too busy raising a family to spend a lot of time raising plants. But as the children grew up and moved out, we began to tackle yard projects with vigor.

First we planted trees and shrubs. The trees we liked most were flowering dogwoods and Japanese maples, which provided beauty without being too big.

Next we dug out grass to make room for curving flower beds. We made an island in the middle of the lawn and planted three rosebushes, 'Mary Rose', 'Summer Snow' and 'Sunsprite'. Over the years, roses became a common feature in our yard.

I also wanted a place to entertain, so Dave designed and built a patio area. He used inexpensive gray and red pavers to create a pattern of 4-foot squares. He left four open squares for plants, which brings the garden right onto the patio. This is especially nice for fragrant flowers.

Our next project came about because we found some free bricks. We decided to use them for another small patio to connect the white dogwood tree to our "rose island." Dave built an arbor beside it, where we planted silver lace vine, which is a lovely focal point when in bloom.

We later started working on a shade garden, planting astilbe, Jacob's ladder, hostas and rhododendrons.

LEARN AS YOU GO

In the beginning, we planted any color of rose or perennial that we liked. Later on, we decided to choose mostly pastels, which created a serene and peaceful atmosphere.

If we see deep-red or orange flowers we really want to try, we put them in our "wild garden" for a season or two. That lets us try them out before adopting them into the rest of our garden.

We've also realized the importance of different shades of green to complement the other hues. One of our favorites for this is lady's mantle (*Alchemilla mollis*), a perennial with large lobed leaves and sprays of tiny greenish-yellow flowers.

We're also more selective about roses. In our early exuberance, we planted about 40 hybrid tea roses. They were beautiful and healthy the first 2 years. The third year, they developed black spot, mildew and rust, and became

BUDGET SECRET:

Nita and Dave built a patio with inexpensive pavers and left squares open for plants, "which brings the garden right onto the patio."

$

Colorful plantings (left) lead to this bench next to a Japanese maple.

infested with aphids.

Now most of our roses are floribundas, shrub roses, rugosas and David Austin English roses. We also have climbing roses like the thornless 'Zephirine Drouhin', graceful 'William Baffin' and 'Dream Weaver'.

ALIVE WITH ACTIVITY

Now that we no longer have to spray roses for diseases, birds visit regularly to feast on aphids and other insects. Birds also flock to our birdbaths and feeders. The hummingbirds have found us, too, along with robins, doves, quail, sparrows, goldfinches and many other species we've yet to identify.

A friend once said visiting our backyard was like being in a park. That really made us feel accomplished, especially considering where we started.

Now we enjoy being able to share our knowledge—and plants—with friends and neighbors. 🌿

Roses and containers surround the Astons' paver-brick patio.

HERE'S THE plan

1. Evergreen
2. Japanese maple
3. Mock orange
4. Rose
5. Patio
6. Sundial
7. Alyssum
8. Butterfly bush
9. Arbor
10. Rhododendron
11. Forget-me-not
12. Hosta
13. Dogwood
14. Perennial garden
15. Bird feeder
16. Birdbath

$ BUDGET SECRET: Why buy expensive topsoil for creating new gardens when you can get it for free? Sue and Dave Johnson of Dallas Center, Iowa requested the excess from a local ditch-digging project. Their only expense: Soil amendments to add nutrients and improve drainage.

best foot
FORWARD

FORGET THE BACKYARD. THESE HOMEOWNERS PUT THEIR BEST STUFF OUT FRONT FOR ALL TO SEE.

BY GEORGE AND RUTH TRAEGER
MELROSE, MINNESOTA

Mother's Day might not arrive here in central Minnesota until spring, but the wait is worth it. As soon as the snow retreats, over 1,000 tulip bulbs burst into bloom in our yard, while numerous shrubs change from drab to dramatic almost overnight.

And that's just the start of the show. As the tulips start to fade, snapdragons, poppies and roses begin to flourish, followed by daylilies, coneflowers, marigolds and more.

My wife, Ruth, and I live on Main Street, right next to the local hospital, and we've made it our mission to keep our flower beds always in bloom. With people constantly passing by our home, it's almost as if our gardening efforts are on display…and we aim to please!

Our yard wasn't always such a centerpiece. It was quite basic when we first bought the property, but Ruth and I could see potential in green grass surrounding our house.

ROOM FOR EXPANSION

At first, we gardened within the confines of our yard. It wasn't long before we ran out of room,

however. My solution? I purchased the empty lot next door so we could spread out.

Now, more than 15 years later, we focus more on maintenance than expansion. We have a dozen planting beds, several ponds and a stream to take care of during the growing season, as well as a 12- by 24-foot greenhouse.

That structure began as a way to compensate for our short growing season. We used it as a place to prepare plants for the garden. Over the course of about 10 years, however, I reconfigured it several times until it reached its present size.

Some of the annuals we tend in the greenhouse go directly into our flower beds. Others are earmarked for the large pots I fill with flowers and set out in the yard. And, because it isn't unusual for temperatures to dip below freezing as late as Memorial Day, I rely on the greenhouse to provide shelter for those containers if frost is in the forecast.

WATER GARDEN PIONEERS

No one else in our small town had a pond when we first decided to install one many years ago, and you can imagine the interest this project generated. The locals regularly asked if they could stop by to see what we'd done.

Those requests keep coming each summer, thanks to the 4,000-gallon pond we put in a few years back. This water feature is stocked with 30 fish, including goldfish and koi, and sports a waterfall, a stream with a bridge and cattails. Geranium-filled planters brighten the banks,

BUDGET SECRET:

Self-sowing plants like cosmos, cleomes and zinnias may not reseed in colder climates. Dee Swanson of Traverse City, Michigan collects seeds as soon as the blooms fade, then dries them indoors. The seeds go in envelopes, which Dee tucks into airtight containers in her fridge until spring.

The Traegers dug this pond and built the footbridge themselves.

while a stately tree surrounded by hostas adds a touch of shade.

Most of our flower beds hold the annuals we cultivate in the greenhouse. Although using annuals means we have to replant each year, the pansies, marigolds, petunias, alyssum and begonias keep our yard brimming with color well into fall.

We've planted many varieties of tulips, which do exceptionally well in this part of the country. By selecting both early- and late-

blooming types, we always have something flowering in spring.

A decorative wrought-iron fence marks the property line between our original yard and the lot we purchased next door, and we use this to support climbing roses, honeysuckle vines and clematis. Yellow, orange and red lilies encircle this spot as well.

Nearby is a garden devoted to roses, and just a few feet away is one my favorite flower beds. This patch is home to 50 or so dahlias that bloom from mid- to late summer. These showy flowers are so amazing. I simply can't get enough of them!

Ensuring that our yard is constantly full of blossoms is a bit of a trick. The key is planning. Ruth and I spend fall and winter plotting out what to grow and where to grow it.

Then we act on those plans when warm weather returns…and before you know it, we're smack dab in the middle of summer, busy deadheading and removing weeds.

Our efforts pay off any time our seven children and 17 grandchildren visit and enjoy the gardens. We also participate in a garden tour and welcome local garden clubs to come see our yard. We've even had tour buses full of vacationers stop by our house.

"I purchased the **empty lot** next door so we could spread out..."

The lush gardens include dahlias; honeysuckle and lilies (above); and hydrangeas (opposite).

See what I mean about our yard being on display?

It's a good thing Ruth and I love planting and pruning, because when you garden on Main Street, everyone pays attention! ❧

BUDGET SECRETS:

Annuals provide season-long color, but buying new plants each year gets expensive. If you use annuals on a grand scale, consider adding a small greenhouse so you can start your own from seed.

$

Jody Reinardy and his wife, Kim, have about 20 gardens at their Hampton, Minnesota home. Expensive? Not at all. Most of their plants are perennials, which spread on their own or have divided and moved. When they do need new plants, garden club sales and farmers' markets are great sources, Jody says.

HERE'S THE plan

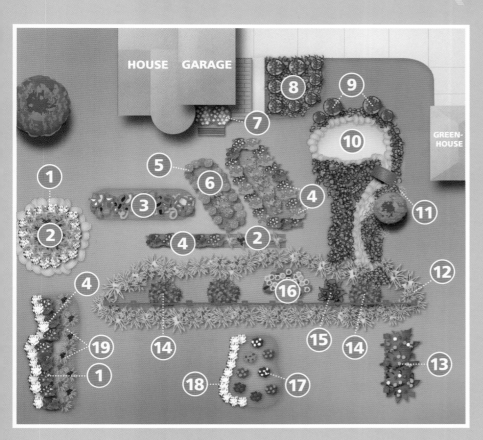

1. Alyssum
2. Tulip
3. Annuals
4. Pansy
5. Begonia
6. Marigold
7. Hydrangea
8. Container garden
9. Geranium
10. Pond
11. Hosta
12. Lily
13. Dahlia
14. Honeysuckle vine
15. Clematis
16. Climbing rose
17. Rose
18. Dusty miller
19. Daylily

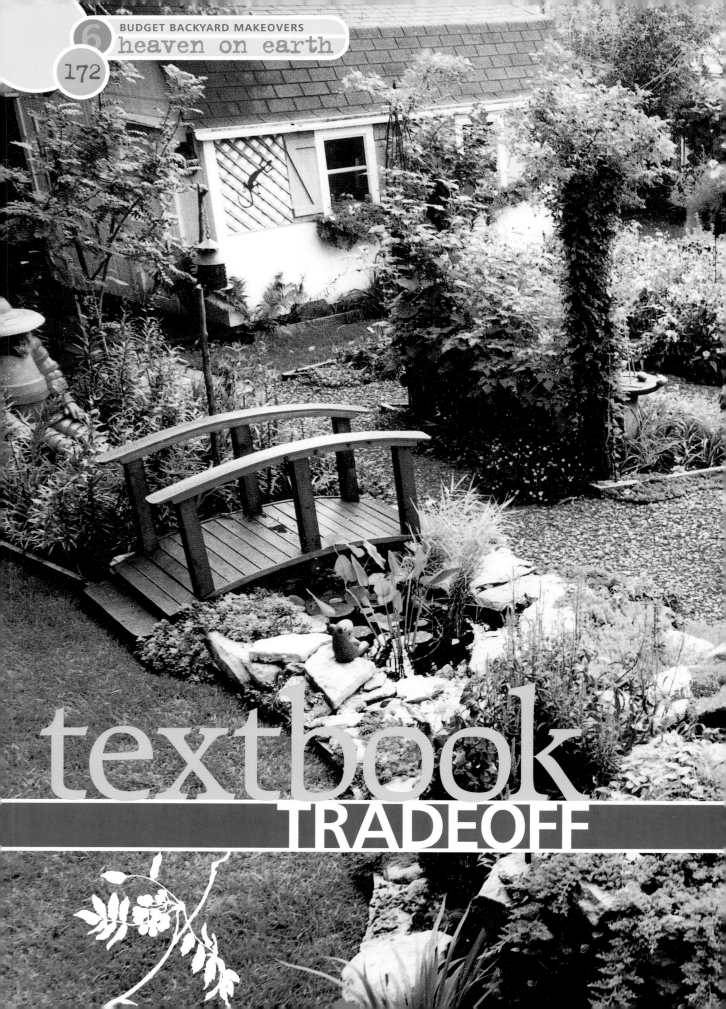

textbook
TRADEOFF

LINDA AND DON PARDIEU
LOUISVILLE, KENTUCKY

MOWING HIS LAWN WAS DRUDGERY.
TENDING HIS GARDENS IS A JOY.

Mowing his yard in the sweltering summer sun gave Don Pardieu a bright idea.

"My plan was to build enough flower beds so I didn't have to cut grass anymore," he chuckles. "Big mistake! I spend a lot more time in the gardens now than the half-hour it took me to mow each week. Luckily I have plenty of time since I retired."

One look at Don's well-tended and flower-filled backyard in Louisville, Kentucky proves he invested that time wisely. The entire sunny portion of his yard is filled with color.

Don started transforming his yard about 20 years ago by building a sweeping back deck. To continue its unique shape, he and his wife, Linda, expanded their vegetable and flower garden to follow the same curve. Then they added triangular beds and crushed-brick paths.

"It became my hobby," Don says. "I gave up golf and decided to spend the money on the yard instead. I've gotten a lot of enjoyment from it."

SEASON-LONG COLOR

The blooming show begins in April, when irises fill what Don calls the "sundial bed." In June, hardy lilies take over, and then bee balm, phlox and yarrow carry color into August and beyond.

"There's not as much upkeep to the gardens as you'd think," Don explains. "We just clean out the beds in spring, top-dress them with some peat moss and add a little 5-5-5 fertilizer to wake the perennials. And the paths help keep everything within reach."

Don's discovered many simple ways to keep his sun-drenched gardens looking lush. During hot weather, he mounts an oscillating wave-type sprinkler atop a 6-foot ladder.

"You wouldn't believe how much farther the sprinkler reaches when you raise it up in the air," he says. "It pretty much takes care of the entire garden area. I only water about once a week."

To keep flowers producing blooms all season, Don religiously deadheads them.

"Anytime a flower fades, I pinch it off and throw it to the ground. I also let some of them reseed. It's a great way to multiply the flowers in your bed and help fill in the empty spaces."

What's next? Maybe a garden for the third of his yard that's covered with heavy shade.

"If I can figure out what to do with it, I won't have to cut any grass," Don jokes. ❦

Don's gardens include fun features like a foot-bridge, pond and the "yard bird" at far right.

"**My plan** was to build enough flower beds so

HERE'S THE plan

1. SUNDIAL BED
    Bearded iris
    Clematis
    Lamb's ear
    Phlox
    Russian sage
    Yarrow
2. "YARD BIRD" BED
    Aster
    Black-eyed Susan
    Daylily
    Foxglove
    Mexican sunflower
    Mountain bluet

3. HUMMINGBIRD BED
    Bee balm
    Lily
    Lavender
    Phlox
    Purple coneflower
4. Hummingbird feeder
5. Birdbath
6. Pergola
7. Vegetable/flower garden
8. Wisteria
9. Rose arbor
10. "Flowerpot man"
11. Bridge
12. Pond

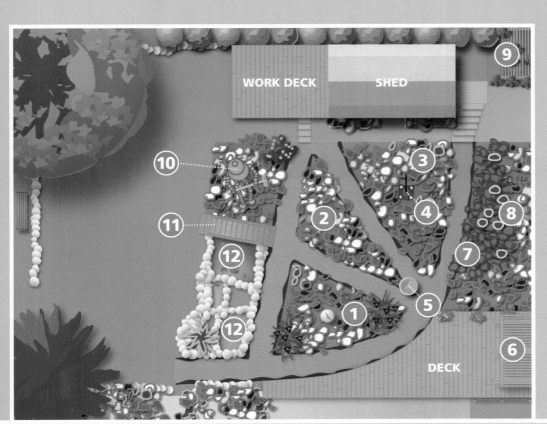

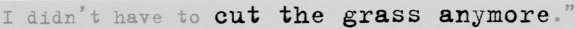

I didn't have to **cut the grass anymore.** "

dressing up
FOR A WEDDING

BY JERRY AND GLADYS HALL
MITCHELL, SOUTH DAKOTA

THEY CREATED A WELL-GROOMED BACKYARD IN TIME FOR THEIR DAUGHTER'S NUPTIALS.

My wife, Gladys, and I remember clear as day when our daughter Erica and son-in-law Chris announced they were marrying. We couldn't have been happier. Then they shocked us.

"We want to get married in your backyard," Erica said.

I couldn't have been more proud or honored. Who wouldn't want their kids, who have such fond memories of home, to spend the most important day of their lives there?

But we never dreamed of a backyard wedding. The idea was almost terrifying. We had a year to get our backyard in shape to make it a "cool place" to get married.

PINING AWAY

Gladys and I always looked to our backyard as a quiet escape from our busy lives. Besides raising three kids, we own and operate two fast-food restaurants, so puttering in the backyard was always a great stress reliever.

When we moved in, we started out with a blank canvas—our lot was barren at best. Since we loved the pines in the beautiful Black Hills of western South Dakota, we decided to bring a bit of that flavor to our backyard in the eastern part of the state.

We planted over 40 pine trees of every variety we could find that would survive the harsh winters—white pine, Black Hills spruce, Colorado blue spruce, ponderosa pine, Austrian pine and a few red cedars.

The biggest trick to planting on a bare lot is to look ahead to the maturity of the trees. You have to envision what an 8-inch tree will look like when it's 40 to 50 feet tall, and not plant trees too close together.

We also had to find a way to keep those trees well watered, because the sandy soil in this area dries out quickly. A neighbor and I got together

BUDGET SECRET:

Watering a sandy 1-1/2-acre lot with city water was "unbelievably expensive," Jerry says, so he and a neighbor dug a well to share. "It was the smartest thing we ever did in the backyard," he says.

and drilled a separate well that we use just for watering. It was the smartest thing we ever did in the backyard. Watering a 1-1/2-acre lot with city water can be unbelievably expensive.

It didn't take too many years to realize we'd need shade trees to keep our lawn green during the hot, dry summers. So we added several varieties of ash, maple, birch and flowering crabapples.

Our landscape continued to develop slowly but surely over the years. We added a sunroom to

HERE'S THE plan

1. Black Hills spruce
2. White pine
3. Mountain ash
4. Birch
5. Mayday tree
6. 'Goldflame' spirea
7. Maple
8. Flowering crabapple
9. Austrian pine
10. Grill area
11. Perennial/annual bed
12. Footbridge
13. Pond
14. Ponderosa pine
15. Colorado blue spruce
16. Gazebo
17. Ash
18. Wedding arbor
19. Linden
20. Arbor
21. "George's Berry Patch"
22. Shed/pumphouse
23. Rhubarb/asparagus garden

replace our deck, then decided to add a garden pond and waterfall just outside it. We couldn't afford the landscaper's estimate, so we decided to do it ourselves. We spent 3 or 4 months on the pond. It was a huge project—just about killed us—but we completed it for $1,000!

A local contractor with a gravel pit saved us tons of money. He had lots of rock set aside, and when I asked how much it would cost to buy some, he replied, "Have at it, buddy."

Over the next several years, we'd planned to build a gazebo, footbridge and arbor, and fix up our existing garden. Now we needed to do all those things before the big day.

I worked every night and weekend for a year to complete those projects, with help from the kids and Gladys. The biggest project, the gazebo, was truly a labor of love. It took most of my spare time over 6 months.

I built the gazebo and arbor from wood I saved from our old deck, which kept costs down. We also incorporated stained glass in the projects, using items recycled from one of our restaurants.

A second arbor covers a brick path leading to "George's Berry Patch," which honors my late father-in-law, who planted our strawberry patch and tended it for many years.

The final touch was connecting the new areas with paver walkways. I had a landscaper do an initial path at the side of the house. After watching him, I decided that job wasn't difficult compared to what we'd already done, so I finished it myself, linking the bridge, grill area and gazebo with rustic walkways.

That year went so fast, I hardly had time to think about what we'd accomplished until after the wedding. It was the most gorgeous outdoor wedding ever...and the bride was beautiful! ❦

> The Mitchells couldn't afford to have a landscaper build a pond, so they did it themselves...for **just $1,000.**

Jerry built the gazebo with wood saved from his old deck.

learning
AS SHE GOES

BY SHARON BRUCK
EARLING, IOWA

NOVICE GARDENER'S KNOWLEDGE GROWS AS HER BACKYARD BLOSSOMS.

When I first started gardening around our country home in southwest Iowa, I was anything but experienced.

Yes, I grew up on a farm, and I can clearly recall my mother's beautiful flower and vegetable beds. But I also remember that working in those gardens was not one of my favorite chores.

Nonetheless, I wholeheartedly plunged into gardening with the help of my husband, Kevin, and our three children, Jessie, Dustin and Luke.

We've been at it for more than 15 years now, and I still learn something new every time I set foot in the backyard.

HERE COMES THE SUN

One of the first large projects we tackled was putting an evergreen windbreak in place of the overgrown grove at the back of the yard. It was a lot of hard work, but the end results were worth it, especially when I discovered that I'd inadvertently created the perfect sunny spot for a garden.

The fact that our yard slopes away from the house provided more lessons in landscaping. Contour planting seemed like the best way to prevent erosion, and I started installing raised beds.

My pennywise ways demanded that I get creative with supplies. Initially, I used low-cost wood chips as mulch, but found them hard on my hands when I tried working in the soil.

So I started tossing the wood chips onto the paths instead. To my surprise, I loved how they set the walking areas apart from the planting beds.

I learned that low-cost or free mulch—ground cornstalk bales and herbicide-free grass clippings, for instance—works just as well in the garden as the more expensive stuff.

I also put old newspapers and cardboard boxes under the mulch, and those materials add even more nutrients to the soil as they break down.

This combination also turned out to be a timesaver, because it retained moisture and kept the weeds down.

BUDGET GARDENING

Growing vegetables for my family to eat was among my first priorities. Then I tried flowers, especially those I could dry and use in arrangements to sell at local craft fairs.

To keep expenses down as my garden grew, I turned to friends and family for cuttings of perennials to fill open spaces.

Today, those beds are bursting with purple coneflowers, rudbeckia, peonies, iris, daylilies, asters, mums, sedum, garden phlox, climbing roses, dianthus, tulips, German statice, yarrow, ferns and more.

Some of these plants are really special, such as the hostas my great-aunt gave me, and the 'Seven Sisters' rose from my parents. The rose came from a plant that's been growing on the family farm for more than 100 years, so it's a real treasure.

I also figured out how to start my own plants indoors from seed, using grow lights in late winter and early spring.

As a result, we have plenty of annuals mixed in with the perennials, including blue salvia, impatiens, alyssum, lobelia, larkspur, zinnias, vinca and geraniums, as well as a healthy assortment of garden vegetables.

KNOWLEDGE TO GROW ON

The flowers and foliage in my garden are varied, but you won't find anything too exotic or unusual here. I know from experience that it's smartest to stick with plants that are hardy in our climate. I also only buy one of each kind, then split the plants as they multiply on

Sharon turned old bedsprings into a trellis and added lots of seating (above and right).

$

BUDGET SECRET:

When creating new garden beds, Sharon surrounds her plants with newspapers and cardboard boxes, then adds a layer of mulch. This not only combats weeds but helps the soil retain moisture—and adds nutrients to the soil as the materials break down. (For Sharon's tip on inexpensive mulch, see page 182.)

their own.

The most important lesson I've learned about this hobby is that there's really no wrong way to go about gardening. Sure, I've made mistakes along the way, but I've also found just as many creative solutions.

And there's nothing more rewarding than taking a walk with my family in this amazing outdoor "classroom" and admiring the results of my green-thumb schooling. 🌿

BUDGET SECRET: $

Instead of buying pricey "designer" mulch for gardens, Sharon looks for free or low-cost materials, like cornstalk bales and herbicide-free grass clippings. "These materials work just as well as the more expensive stuff," she says.

HERE'S THE plan

1. Hosta
2. Bench
3. Impatiens
4. Strawberry patch
5. Peony
6. Vegetable garden
7. Evergreen
8. German statice
9. Phlox
10. Black-eyed Susan
11. Daylily
12. Birdhouse
13. 'Goldflame' spirea
14. 'Seven Sisters' rose
15. Stump with petunias
16. Lily

THE FRUGAL gardener

HER DIRT-CHEAP METHODS WILL SAVE YOU PLENTY OF GREEN.

**KAREN MATTHEWS
ADAMS, MASSACHUSETTS**

My yard blooms with rare and unusual plants that look expensive but didn't cost me much. You can have glorious gardens, too—without emptying your pocketbook.

A great way to start is to grow plants from seed and then harvest seeds from those plants for next year. This is very economical because I only have to purchase the seeds once. I choose top-quality seeds from a reliable company. Spending a few cents more on good seeds is a wise investment. It saves you from worrying about poor germination or inferior plants.

I also choose plants that "come true" from seed. This means avoiding hybrids that may not produce offspring the same as their parents.

When my plants bloom, I mark the prettiest flowers on the healthiest plants with a colored twist tie or piece of yarn. This makes harvesting the best seeds easier once they ripen.

Another tip: Don't be reluctant to stop when you see someone working in their yard to tell them how much you admire their gardens. Most gardeners are proud to show off their efforts, and some may snip off a piece of a plant or offer a seedling for you to take home. Many shrubs and perennials can be started this way. It's even easier and cheaper than seeds!

But I think swapping is the best way to get expensive or hard-to-find plants. Plants like irises (left), hostas and daylilies (lower left) are easy to divide, so they're great to swap.

Of course, to get someone to share a division of prize iris, you'll need to have something equally tempting to offer in return.

To ensure this, I only buy really special plants that are easy to propagate. Although they tend to be expensive at first, I know I'll get my money back several times.

Also, don't forget about local garden clubs. They are wonderful places to connect with gardeners who may want to share their plants with others.

Try these ideas and, before long, you'll have an impressive collection of plants—and barely a dent in your wallet. 🌾

BUDGET SECRET:

$ "Swapping is the best way to get plants that are hard to find or expensive," Karen says. "Daylilies, iris and hosta are easy to divide, so they're great to swap."

BRIGHTideas

DIVINE...ON A DIME

Shared plants, recycled items and homemade garden
structures give these gardens their own heavenly appeal.

tribute to grandma Lyda
Behnke patterned her gardens
in Mount Shasta, California after
those at her grandmother's ranch.
Husband Rusty built this nostalgic
arbor, which Lyda dressed up with
clematis and climbing roses. Rusty
used wood salvaged from the ranch
to make fencing, and turned
remnants, like an old milk cart,
into flower containers.

inviting entryway
This attractive recycling
project in Rose Reuber's
yard in Bow Island, Alberta
turned trash into treasure.
Rose gathered old fence
posts and corral posts to
make a new entryway for
her garden.

rock on! A neighbor's old rocker was headed for the trash pile until Darlene Price's husband salvaged it. He replaced the seat with a "hanging basket" of chicken wire and hardware cloth, and Darlene added potting soil and impatiens. "It makes a great focal point," says Darlene of Roswell, Georgia. "Another neighbor threw out a ladder-back chair with a broken cane seat, and I'm going to fix that one up, too."

curb appeal An annual citywide gardening contest didn't just prod Buffalo, New York residents to spruce up their front yards. It also inspired them to start sharing plants and seeds, making the beautification effort more economical for all. Sandy Whitt took her front yard to new heights with cleome and a vine-covered arbor.

garden gnomes welcome! "We call this garden gate our 'gnome door,'" says Jill Monczunski of Brighton, Michigan. "Using an old door was my husband's idea. He installed it—minus the window glass, so it's safe for children—and I added the painting. It's become a real conversation piece, and my neighbors and I have had lots of laughs decorating it."

BUDGET-WISE SHOWSTOPPERS

ZINNIA
ZINNIA ELEGANS

Bloom time: Summer to fall.

Light needs: Full sun.

Hardiness: Annual.

Mature plant size: 6 inches to 4 feet high, 6 inches to 2 feet wide.

Care tip: Full sun is best; if mildew is a problem, grow one of the newer resistant varieties.

BUTTERFLY BUSH
BUDDLEIA SPECIES AND CULTIVARS

Bloom time: Late spring through late summer.

Light needs: Full sun.

Hardiness: Zones 5 or 6 to 9.

Mature plant size: 4 to 8 feet high and wide.

Care tip: Cut back in early spring. Attracts lots of bees and butterflies!

BLACK-EYED SUSAN, GLORIOSA DAISY
RUDBECKIA SPECIES AND CULTIVARS

Bloom time: Midsummer to fall.

Light needs: Full sun.

Hardiness: Zones 3 to 10.

Mature plant size: 2 to 3 feet high and wide.

Care tip: Ordinary soil and full sun bring out the best in this stalwart.

COLEUS
COLEUS HYBRIDS

Bloom time: Summer.

Light needs: Full sun to partial shade.

Hardiness: Annual.

Mature plant size: Up to 3 to 4 feet high and wide.

Care tip: Better, longer-lasting color in partial to full shade.

JAPANESE BLOOD GRASS
IMPERATA CYLINDRICA

Bloom time: Summer to fall.

Light needs: Full sun.

Hardiness: Zones 5 to 9.

Mature plant size: 1 to 2 feet high and wide.

Care tip: Provide an open spot with fertile soil or grow in large container, such as a half whiskey barrel.

WHEN YOU WANT SOMETHING SPECTACULAR IN YOUR GARDEN, LOOK TO PLANTS THAT AREN'T JUST BOLD AND SPLASHY, BUT RESILIENT, SO YOU WON'T NEED TO REPLACE THEM ANYTIME SOON. WE LOVE THESE LOW-COST SHOWSTOPPERS.

BLUEBEARD, BLUE MIST SHRUB

CARYOPTERIS X CLANDONENSIS

Bloom time: Mid- to late summer.

Light needs: Full sun.

Hardiness: Zones 6 to 9.

Mature plant size: 2 to 3 feet high, 3 feet or more wide.

Care tip: Cut back in late winter. Overly fertile soil leads to rampant growth.

SHASTA DAISY

LEUCANTHEMUM X SUPERBUM

Bloom time: Summer to fall.

Light needs: Full sun to partial shade.

Hardiness: Zones 5 to 9.

Mature plant size: 1 to 3 feet high, 2 feet wide.

Care tip: Looks better and is more productive when grown in fertile, well-drained soil and watered consistently.

CLEOME, SPIDER FLOWER

CLEOME HASSLERIANA

Bloom time: Summer.

Light needs: Full to partial sun.

Hardiness: Annual.

Mature plant size: 3 to 5 feet high, 1 to 2 feet wide.

Care tip: To prevent reseeding, cut flowers for bouquets before seedheads form.

'KNOCK OUT' ROSE

ROSA CULTIVAR

Bloom time: Summer.

Light needs: Full sun.

Hardiness: Zones 4 to 9.

Mature plant size: 3 to 4 feet high, 3 feet wide.

Care tip: Though extraordinarily tough and prolific, it needs regular watering, in-season fertilizing and deadheading.

RUSSIAN SAGE

PEROVSKIA ATRIPLICIFOLIA

Bloom time: Midsummer to fall.

Light needs: Full sun.

Hardiness: Zones 5 to 7.

Mature plant size: 2 to 4 feet high and wide.

Care tip: Cut back low in fall or early spring to encourage new growth.

simplest bench
IN THE WORLD

$ BUILDING TIPS:

To make a simple project even simpler, remember these tips:

- Be sure to assemble the legs (Step 2) so they're mirror images of each other, and not facing the same direction.

- Use clamps or a helper to hold the legs upright when securing the seat.

- Predrill all screw holes to prevent splitting the wood.

BY JEAN BARTHOLOME, DURANGO, COLORADO

One of the easiest ways to make a good garden even better is to set a comfortable bench in a secluded corner. Just having a place to sit transforms an ordinary patch of flowers into a quiet, contemplative refuge.

When I was looking for a simple bench, I remembered hearing about a useful design once built by Aldo Leopold. Many consider him the father of wildlife ecology, and his writings celebrate what it means to live in harmony with the land. If this bench was good enough for him, it's definitely good enough for me!

A little research led me to this sturdy design I could build quickly with a few 2x8s, glue and screws. Best of all, it's amazingly comfortable and perfect for bird-watching—even for two people. Thanks, Aldo!

WHAT YOU NEED:

- ☐ Speed square or protractor
- ☐ Drill with #8 countersink drill bit
- ☐ Circular saw
- ☐ Caulking gun
- ☐ 1 2x8 x 8 cedar, redwood or treated lumber (seat and backrest)
- ☐ 1 2x8 x 10 cedar, redwood or treated lumber (front and rear legs)
- ☐ Exterior construction adhesive
- ☐ 2-1/2" galvanized deck screws

BUILD YOUR OWN BENCH

① Mark one end of the 2x8 x 10 at a 22-1/2-degree angle with a speed square or protractor, then cut with a circular saw. Make a mark 36 inches away and repeat the cut at the same angle. Cut the remaining front leg and two back legs from the same piece. Cut the seat and the backrest from the 2x8 x 8.

22½-DEGREE READING

② Fasten the legs together. Stack and clamp the seat and backrest to the edge of the worktable as guides, then align the legs against them. Spread adhesive on the front leg, set the rear leg in place, and fasten the legs together with three 2-1/2-inch screws.

LEG ASSEMBLY

17¼"

③ Attach the seat and backrest. Stand the two ends up, 42 inches apart, spread glue on the tops of the rear legs, and screw the seat in place. Lay the bench on the worktable and attach the backrest with glue and screws.

2½" SCREWS

45"

17¼"

42"

36"

Photo Credits

Front cover: Gary Mottau

CHAPTER 1

Pages 6-7: Gay Bumgarner

Pages 22-23: Amber Cook

Page 26: Stemach garden, Thomas Hallstein

Page 28: pansy, RDA Inc.; lady's mantle, RDA Inc.; flowering maple, RDA Inc.; 'Easy Wave' pink petunia, Ball Horticultural Co.; Japanese painted fern, RDA Inc.

Page 29: calibrachoa, RDA Inc.; lavender, RDA Inc.; pink, David Cavagnaro; feverfew, RDA Inc.; coralbells, David Cavagnaro

CHAPTER 2

Pages 30-31: Irene Jeruss

Pages 32-33: Joyce Bambach

Page 34: barn and garden photo at lower right, Joyce Bambach

Pages 40-42: Gary Mottau

Pages 48-50: Bonnie Nance

Page 58: Bill Zuehlke

Page 59: photos, Bill Zuehlke; illustration, Frank Rohrbach

Pages 60-61: HSP

Page 64: 'Red Flare' waterlily, Albert Squillace/Positive Images; 'Tropicana' canna, Aquascape Designs

Page 65: water lettuce, Diane A Pratt/Positive Images; lotus, Michael Lustbader/The Image Finders

CHAPTER 3

Pages 66-67: Irene Jeruss

Pages 76-77: Jim Wieland/RP Photo

Page 79: Jim Wieland/RP Photo

Page 91: Bill Zuehlke

Page 93: Kathy Bomey garden, Vivette Botner

Page 95: milk cart, Mark Turner; wagon, Mark Turner

Page 96: California poppy, Susan Muri; morning glory, Gene Kunz; cosmos, Rick Waybright; impatiens, RDA Inc.; nasturtium, Nancy Rotenberg

Page 97: hosta, Netherlands Flower Bulb Info Center; bugleweed, RDA Inc.; lily, Nancy C. Friend; windflower, Pam Spaulding/

Positive Images; dahlia, Netherlands Flower Bulb Info Center

CHAPTER 4

Pages 98-99: Gay Bumgarner

Pages 108-109: Thomas Hallstein/Outsight

Page 111: garden view through arch, Thomas Hallstein/Outsight; planting cavities and patio, Brian Barron

Page 120: Scheuch/Hajek garden, Mark Turner

Page 122: daylily, Jerry Rabideau; cotoneaster, RDA Inc.; wild rose, David Cavagnaro; English ivy, RDA Inc.; pachysandra, David Cavagnaro

Page 123: rosemary, RDA Inc.; periwinkle, RDA Inc.; Japanese barberry, RDA Inc.; Hall's honeysuckle, RDA Inc.; ice plant, David Cavagnaro

Page 124: RP Photos

CHAPTER 5

Pages 126-127: Bonnie Nance

Pages 128-130: Ramona Boone

Page 142: Nancy Matthews

Page 143: Susan and Bill Moyer, Nancy Matthews

Page 144: garden path, Nancy Matthews

Pages 146-149: John Robert Williams

Page 152: all plant photos, RDA Inc.

Page 153: blue oat grass, Ann Reilly/Positive Images; Iceland poppy, RDA Inc.; peony, RDA Inc.; serviceberry, RDA Inc.; blazing star, RDA Inc.

Page 154: RP Photo

CHAPTER 6

Pages 156-157: Priscilla Valle garden, Alan and Linda Detrick

Pages 158-160: Grace Natoli Sheldon/RP Photo

Page 179: gazebo, Greg Latza

Page 183: iris, Linda S. Mitchell; daylily, Ann Kulig

Page 186: zinnia, Denise Hussey; butterfly bush, RDA Inc.; black-eyed Susan, Ann Kulig; coleus, RDA Inc.; Japanese blood grass, RDA Inc.

Page 187: bluebeard, RDA Inc.; Shasta daisy, RDA Inc.; cleome, Irene Jeruss; 'Knock Out' rose, Peter A. Hogg/Monrovia; Russian sage, RDA Inc.

Page 188: bench, Mike Krivit

What's Inside...

Plan Your Best Garden Ever!

By Teri Dunn, Gloucester, Massachusetts

T is the season for gardening resolutions. You may miss the garden you had last year…or miss the garden you *wish* you'd had. But winter's respite is not the time for regrets. Instead, make good use of the off-season. Grab pencil, paper, gardening magazines and seed catalogs, and make your dream garden a reality!

To help you along, we've compiled some useful tips, plant recommendations and no-fail garden plans. As you imagine your future garden, bear in mind the wisdom of this old saying: "Don't work harder – work smarter."

RDA INC.

How to use our tips:

Don't worry about trying all these ideas or using them in order or in the winter months. Springtime's arrival in your area and the scope of your plans will guide you to the ones most useful to you.

1 Set aside a large-format wall calendar just for gardening notes. Use it for goals, several-step garden projects and timely reminders.

2 Shop early for containers, well before buying plants to fill them. There will be a bigger selection, and you can make cool-headed decisions.

3 Inventory your seed stash. Improperly stored seeds may have dried out and should be discarded. Be sure to store seeds in an airtight jar in the refrigerator.

>> 3 Inventory your seed stash. Improperly stored seeds may have dried out.

4 Clean your hand tools now, while you have time. Chip off encrusted dirt and rub with a damp rag. Then wipe cutting surfaces with an oily cloth.

5 Review plant information in catalogs and gardening magazines. Resolve to try something new this year, and decide now where it will go in your garden.

6 Cruise through catalogs with a marker and/or yellow sticky notes, flagging everything you might want to order. You can always pare down the list later.

7 When ordering seeds or plants via mail order, fill out the order form (even if you intend to call in your order or use the Internet). This way, you are prepared and the process goes quickly.

8 Place orders early, before the companies get busy. These get filled faster, plus you can get exactly what you want, thus avoiding substitutions and rain checks.

9 Stockpile soil amendments. Order or buy loam, compost and mulch weeks before you need them. When you do, they'll be there.

10 Plan new beds and borders on paper. The drawing

>> 4 Clean your hand tools now.

>> 10 Plan new beds on paper.

ILLUSTRATION: LARRY MIKEC

>> 2 Shop early for containers, while there is still a wide selection.

DEREK FELL

>> **15** Line up contractors early if you plan to install a water garden, gazebo or pergola.

it's still important to know what to expect to allow for enough space.

12 Call your nearest cooperative extension office and ask when the last predicted frost-free date is, or check on-line. This information will help you calculate how early to start seeds indoors.

13 Start seeds of some of your favorite veggies and annuals indoors several weeks or months in advance. This way, seedlings can go right into the garden without delay when conditions are warm enough.

14 Sketch a new plan for your vegetable garden. It's important to rotate crops in order to thwart plant-specific pests and diseases. It also gives the soil a break because different plants use more or less of certain nutrients.

15 If you're planning a big garden installation this year – a water garden, a gazebo, a pergola – research what's involved. Also, line up contractors in late winter (before they book up).

16 Tour the yard with a sharp pair of clippers. Make way for new growth by removing deadwood, winter-damaged branches and suckers. If in doubt about whether a branch is alive, spare it for now.

17 Feed developing seedlings with half-strength plant food every week or so. Proper care means more robust plants, improving their chances of survival when they finally move outdoors.

doesn't have to be sophisticated or perfect, though you should aim to make it to scale.

11 For new plants, always research "mature plant size." Of course, results may vary in your garden, but

18 Plant bare-root shrubs and perennials earlier in the spring than container-grown plants. Bare-root ones are still dormant or just waking up and can make a gradual transition to garden life.

19 How do you know when it's okay to start planting? Check the soil – just scoop up a handful and squeeze it. If it's wet and soggy, wait a bit longer. If it crumbles in your hands, it's time.

20 Help acclimate young plants before they go into the ground. Set pots and flats in a sheltered spot (under a tree, on the porch) and gradually increase light received for a week or so – bring them in at night or cover them if frost is predicted.

21 Lay a garden hose on the ground to visualize the size and shape of a new garden bed. Leave it in place for a few days, so you can observe it from various angles and at different times of the day (to check sunlight).

22 To plant a shrub or rosebush, dig a hole that is the same depth as but wider than the root-ball. Backfill with a mix of organic matter and existing soil.

23 When buying perennials or annuals, resist the temptation to get blooming plants. A strong root system is much more important and will soon generate good top growth and flowers.

24 Get in the habit of creating a basin around the outer edges of every plant you install, large or small. When you water, precious moisture won't drain away but will go right to the root zone.

25 Groom emerging perennials, cutting out last year's tangled growth. This not only makes them look a lot better, but clears the way for fresh, new growth.

26 Plant in threes. This classic rule of thumb really works — it gives plants an opportunity to make an impression, yet not hog the garden stage. Plus, the odd number looks more natural.

27 Make compost! It's easy and it's free…and your plants will adore it. The most successful piles are in a sunny spot, about 3 feet square. Keep compost slightly damp and stir often.

28 Set out a rain barrel in a convenient, but out-of-the way, spot (usually under a downspout). Cover it with a screen to keep out leaves, dirt and mosquitoes.

29 Where grass meets flower bed, create a shallow trench bordering the garden. Fill it with gravel or edging material if you wish. Ideally, it will halt the grass, as well as encroaching weeds.

>> **27** Make compost. It's easy, and your plants will love it!

>> **13** Start some of your favorite veggies indoors from seed.

RP PHOTO

30 When it's in its prime, evaluate your spring bulb display. Take photos; make notes. Tuck this information away till later in the summer, when you can move bulbs and order new ones.

>> 30
Evaluate your spring bulb display when it's in its prime.

31 Fight weeds early and often. They're easier to pull out by the roots after a rain or after you water. Crowds of small ones can be cut out with a few swipes of a sharp hoe.

32 Add some quick color to your garden. Cold-tolerant annuals are great for filling the mid- to late-spring gaps – dependable favorites include pansies and snapdragons.

33 Always fully prepare a new bed before planting. Get all weeds, roots and rocks out first. Then dig the soil to a depth of 6 to 8 inches, at least, incorporating plenty of good organic matter.

34 Newly installed transplants appreciate a little protection from sun and wind at first. Use cardboard boxes, "row cover" fabric or even a carefully placed lawn chair.

*3 no-fail garden plans

New lot? Freshening up an existing landscape? Whatever your plans hold for this spring, you can't go wrong with these easy-to plant, even easier-to-care-for garden design ideas. You're virtual guaranteed success, whether you have full sun…or none!

plan 1 DROUGHT-TOLERANT, SUNNY BORDER

This pretty border garden features tough plants that thrive in less-than-ideal conditions.

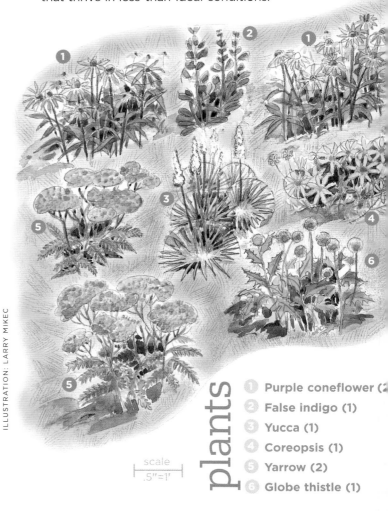

scale
.5"=1'

plants
1 Purple coneflower (2
2 False indigo (1)
3 Yucca (1)
4 Coreopsis (1)
5 Yarrow (2)
6 Globe thistle (1)

Globe thistle

Globe thistle
Botanical name: *Echinops ritro.*
Hardiness: Zones 3 to 8.
Height/Spread: 3 to 4 feet tall/2 to 3 feet wide.
Light needs: Full sun.
Flower color: Blue.
Care tip: Flower color is more intense in full sun...and if nights are cooler.
Why it's a winner: Unique-looking flower with great color.

Yarrow

Yarrow
Botanical name: *Achillea* species and cultivars.
Hardiness: Zones 3 to 8.
Height/Spread: 1 to 2 feet tall and wide; some larger.
Light needs: Full sun.
Flower color: Varies; a mix is fun.
Care tip: Average, well-draining soil is ideal.
Why it's a winner: Easy to grow (some reseed) and colorful.

Purple coneflower
Botanical name: *Echinacea purpurea.*
Hardiness: Zones 3 to 8.
Height/Spread: 2 to 4 feet tall/2 feet wide.
Light needs: Full sun.
Flower color: Purple with orange center.
Care tip: Well-drained soil is a must; struggles in damp sites.
Why it's a winner: Prolific and reliable.

False indigo
Botanical name: *Baptisia australis.*
Hardiness: Zones 3 to 9.
Height/Spread: 3 to 4 feet tall/4 feet wide.
Light needs: Full sun.
Flower color: Dark blue.
Care tip: Develops a taproot, so plant where you want it...and leave it there.
Why it's a winner: After pretty flowers pass, foliage and plant form remain very attractive.

False indigo

Yucca
Botanical name: *Yucca filamentosa.*
Hardiness: Zones 4 to 10.
Height/Spread: 2 to 3 feet tall and wide (flower stalk to 6 or more feet tall).
Light needs: Full sun.
Flower color: White bells.
Care tip: If "pups" (offsets) develop, separate and plant them in the spring.

Coreopsis

Yucca

Why it's a winner: Dramatic both in and out of flower.

Coreopsis
Botanical name: *Coreopsis* species and cultivars.
Hardiness: Zones 3 to 9.
Height/Spread: 1 to 3 feet tall/2 feet wide.
Light needs: Full sun.
Flower color: Yellow daisies.
Care tip: Deadhead to encourage more flowers.
Why it's a winner: Many cultivars are always blooming; loose, casual profile.

Purple coneflower

SPECIAL BONUS SECTION!

ALAN AND LINDA DETRICK

ALAN AND LINDA DETRICK

RDA INC.

RDA INC.

ANNE GORDON/ANNE GORDON IMAGES

✳ plan 2

CURVY, ALL-SUMMER COLOR BED

Vibrant, long-lasting bloomers are the stars of this showstopping garden.

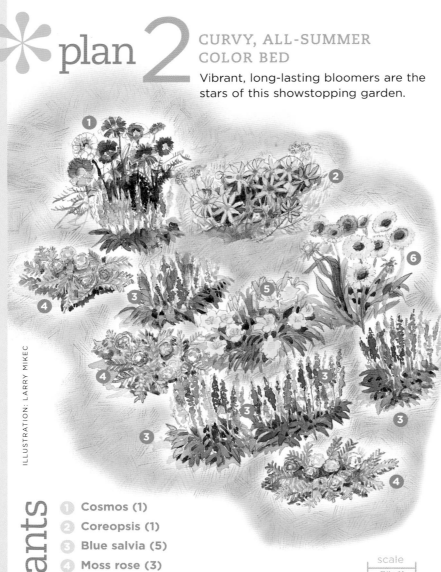

Moss rose

ILLUSTRATION: LARRY MIKEC

plants

1. Cosmos (1)
2. Coreopsis (1)
3. Blue salvia (5)
4. Moss rose (3)
5. 'Stella d'Oro' daylily (1)
6. Blanket flower (1)

scale
.5"=1'

Cosmos

DAVID CAVAGNARO

Height/Spread: Up to 8 inches tall spreading habit.
Light needs: Full sun.
Flower color: Red, orange, pink, yellow, white; single or double blooms.
Care tip: Well-drained or drier soil better; falters in wet ground.
Why it's a winner: Though low-growing, it grabs attention with its perky colors.

Coreopsis *(pictured on page 33)*
Botanical name:
Coreopsis species and cultivars.
Hardiness: Zones 3 to 9.
Height/Spread: 1 to 3 feet tall/2 feet wide.
Light needs: Full sun.
Flower color: Yellow daisy-like blooms
Care tip: Avoid overly rich soils, which promote floppy growth.
Why it's a winner: Many cultivars are always blooming; loose, casual profile

Cosmos

Botanical name: *Cosmos bipinnatus.*
Hardiness: Annual.
Height/Spread: 1 to 6 feet tall/1 to 2 feet wide (there are dwarf types).
Light needs: Full sun.
Flower color: A variety of hues – pink, white and red; mixes are great.
Care tip: Too-rich soil leads to poor flower production and floppy plants.
Why it's a winner: Always in bloom; always looks terrific.

Moss rose

Botanical name:
Portulaca grandiflora.
Hardiness: Annual.

Blanket flower

Blanket flower
Botanical name:
Gaillardia species and cultivars.
Hardiness: Zones 3 to 8.
Height/Spread: 1 to 3 feet tall and wide
Light needs: Full sun.

'Stella d'Oro' daylily

Flower color: Red-and-yellow daisy-shaped flower.
Care tip: Prefers well-drained soil; damp ground and heavy clay are fatal.
Why it's a winner: Gorgeous and utterly dependable.

'Stella d'Oro' daylily

Botanical name: *Hemerocallis* cultivar.
Hardiness: Zones 3 to 9.
Height/Spread: 1 to 1-1/2 feet tall and wide.
Light needs: Full sun to part shade.
Flower color: Golden yellow trumpets.
Care tip: Has a sweet fragrance, so position where you can enjoy it.
Why it's a winner: Dwarf plant is especially long-blooming.

Blue salvia

Botanical name: *Salvia farinacea.*
Hardiness: Annual.
Height/Spread: Up to 3 feet tall/1 foot wide.
Light needs: Full to partial sun.
Flower color: Violet-blue spires.
Care tip: Needs average to fertile soil that is well drained; some shelter from blazing afternoon sun is good.
Why it's a winner: Great source of dependable violet-blue spires.

Blue salvia

35 Invest in a watering wand. This hose-end attachment delivers a soft, soaking spray that young plants appreciate (it's also terrific for watering hanging baskets).

36 Get in the habit of protecting newly installed plants with an inch or two of mulch. This helps moderate summer's high soil temperatures, retains soil moisture and keeps weeds at bay.

Mulch around newly installed plants.

37 Clip flowers off your spring-flowering shrubs (lilacs, rhododendrons, azaleas, spirea and the like) as they begin to fade. It helps the plant conserve energy, plus it just looks better.

38 When watering larger plants or trees, set a hose at the base on slow trickle. Check back periodically, and turn it off for a bit if there's too much runoff. The idea is to give them a deep soaking.

39 Put in a ground cover! Clear out an area and dig in organic matter to a depth of several inches. Stagger the plants rather than make rows. Don't plant too closely – they'll fill in.

40 The best way to fertilize shrubs and rosebushes is with slow-release granular plant food. Follow label directions about timing and amount. Always water before and after for maximum uptake.

41 The secrets to a great focal-point planting? Choose a large-growing plant that looks good from all angles. Elevate it and/or surround it with lower-growers. Finally, be sure to pick a color that contrasts with its surroundings.

42 To make a great window box display, hold a "dress rehearsal" first – set potted plants inside and shift them around until you are satisfied you have enough and that they are well placed.

43 Prevent lawn-mowing challenges. Elevate garden decor items on level paving blocks or stepping-stones. This applies not only to potted plants, but also urns, birdbaths, benches or sundials.

44 For vines and climbers, put in stakes or other supports as early as possible – at planting time or soon after. This prevents puncturing the root-ball, plus it reminds you to keep after the tying. Redirect or prune back wayward stems.

>> 44 Tie climbing plants to supports as early as possible.

>> 45
Deadhead perennials and annuals.

45 Deadhead all perennials and annuals that don't shed spent flowers on their own. This simple chore persuades plants to direct their energy into producing more blooms (rather than going to seed).

46 Prevent plant diseases and insect damage by keeping your plants tidy. Get rid of damaged growth and yellowing leaves— clip them off the plant and, just as important, rake them out and away from underneath.

47 Spring is the best time to prune, shear or shape your backyard evergreens, whether they are solo performers or part of a hedge. It's important that you use a good, sharp tool for this kind of job.

✳ plan 3

SHADY, CORNER BED

You can count on these plants to brighten up most any shadowy spot.

scale
.5"=1'

plants

1. Solomon's seal (1)
2. Bleeding heart (2)
3. Yellow wax-bells (1)
4. Sweet woodruff (2)
5. Astilbe (5)

Bleeding heart

Bleeding heart
Botanical name: *Dicentra spectabilis*
Hardiness: Zones 2 to 9.
Height/Spread: 1 to 3 feet tall and wide.
Light needs: Partial to full shade.
Flower color: Little pink-and-white lockets.
Care tip: Goes dormant when summer gets hot and dry...cut it back then.
Why it's a winner: Long bloom period in spring; attractive, ferny foliage.

Sweet woodruff
Botanical name: *Galium odoratum.*
Hardiness: Zones 4 to 8.
Height/Spread: Up to 6 inches tall; has spreading habit.
Light needs: Partial to full shade.
Flower color: Little white stars.

48 Open your garden to more light and air with springtime pruning if needed. Remove a few of the lower branches of tall trees, thin overgrown trees and shrubs and take out branches that are invading garden areas.

49 Check the effectiveness of your watering methods. Right after you turn off the hose or sprinkler, dig down with a trowel to see how far the moisture penetrated into the soil – you may be surprised.

50 Splashy and dependable color is easy – use potted plants. Move them in and out of displays as needed. Just remember: Don't neglect watering, as containers dry out quickly. ❧

>>50 Use potted plants for easy color.

DAVID CAVAGNARO

Sweet woodruff

Care tip: Rein in if it spreads too far.
Why it's a winner: A great "weaver" among taller plants.

Yellow wax-bells
Botanical name: *Kirengshoma palmata.*
Hardiness: Zones 4 to 8.

Yellow wax-bells

Height/Spread: 2 to 4 feet tall/2 to 3 feet wide.
Light needs: Partial to full shade.
Flower color: Yellow bells.
Care tip: Give it moist, well-drained soil and some shelter from winds.
Why it's a winner: Abundant yellow flowers in late summer to fall.

Astilbe
Botanical name:
Astilbe species and cultivars.
Hardiness: Zones 4 to 9.
Height/Spread: 2 to 4 feet tall/2 feet wide.
Light needs: Partial shade, partial sun.
Flower color: White, red, purple, or pink spires.
Care tip: Soil must be sufficiently and consistently moist.
Why it's a winner: Contributes color during slow periods in a shade garden.

Solomon's seal
Botanical name:
Polygonatum biflorum.
Hardiness: Zones 3 to 9.
Height/Spread: 2 to 3 feet tall and wide.
Light needs: Partial to full shade.
Flower color: Tiny white bells.
Growing or care tip: Beware of slugs and snails! Handpick or set out traps.
Why it's a winner: It's a graceful choice for standing behind shorter plants.

Astilbe

PHOTOS, BELOW AND LEFT: RDA INC.

Solomon's seal

Plant Hardiness Zone Map

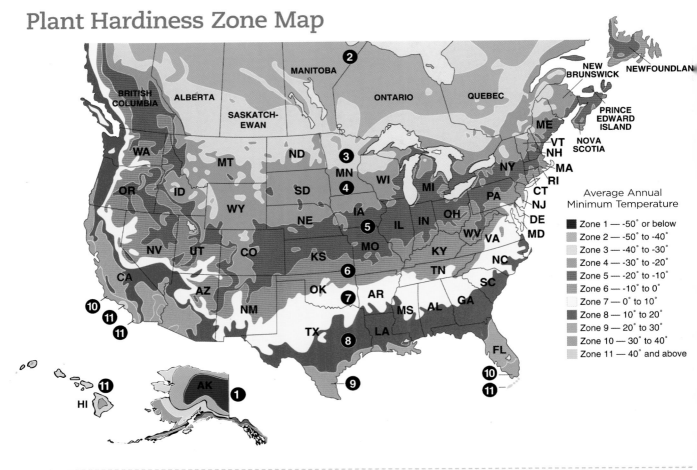

Average Annual Minimum Temperature

- Zone 1 — -50° or below
- Zone 2 — -50° to -40°
- Zone 3 — -40° to -30°
- Zone 4 — -30° to -20°
- Zone 5 — -20° to -10°
- Zone 6 — -10° to 0°
- Zone 7 — 0° to 10°
- Zone 8 — 10° to 20°
- Zone 9 — 20° to 30°
- Zone 10 — 30° to 40°
- Zone 11 — 40° and above

Plant Heat-Zone Map

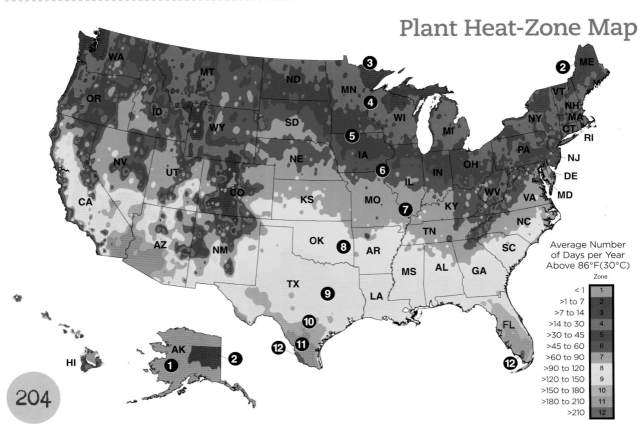

Average Number of Days per Year Above 86°F(30°C)

	Zone
< 1	1
>1 to 7	2
>7 to 14	3
>14 to 30	4
>30 to 45	5
>45 to 60	6
>60 to 90	7
>90 to 120	8
>120 to 150	9
>150 to 180	10
>180 to 210	11
>210	12

Garden Journal

Use this page to record important information about your own backyard makeover. Keep track of plant names, planting dates in your area, must-do garden tasks and any tips you learn along the way.

Backyard Planning Grid

Sketch your backyard makeover ideas right onto this handy grid paper, or make photocopies to accomodate hundreds of garden plan possibilities. After all, you're only limited by your imagination!

SCALE: ¼″ = 1′

Itemized Budget Estimator

Stay on budget with this handy tally sheet. Just fill in material and labor costs, and you'll have an itemized, at-a-glance overview of your backyard makeover.

ITEM	QUANTITY x	UNIT COST =	ITEM COST	LABOR	TOTAL
	x	=			
	x	=			
	x	=			
	x	=			
	x	=			
	x	=			
	x	=			
	x	=			
	x	=			
	x	=			
	x	=			
	x	=			
	x	=			
	x	=			
	x	=			
	x	=			
	x	=			
	x	=			
	x	=			

Total item cost _____   **Total labor cost** _____   **Total item & labor cost** ____

Additional Notes